Editor: Donna Wood
Art Editor: Alison Fenton
Picture Researcher: Alice Earle
Proofreader: Judith Forshaw
Indexer: Marie Lorimer
Cartography provided by the Mapping Services Department of AA Publishing
Image retouching and colour repro: Sarah Montgomery
Production: Nathan Clark

Produced by AA Publishing
© AA Media Limited 2011. Reprinted 2015.

Published by AA Publishing (a trading name of AA Media Limited, whose
registered office is Fanum House, Basing View, Basingstoke, Hampshire
RG21 4EA; registered number 06112600).

Contains Ordnance Survey data © Crown copyright and database right 2015

A05387

ISBN: 978-0-7495-7696-7

A CIP catalogue record for this book is available from the British Library.

The contents of this book are believed correct at the time of printing.
Nevertheless, the publishers cannot be held responsible for any errors or
omissions or for changes in the details given in this book or for the consequences
of any reliance on the information provided by the same. This does not affect your
statutory rights.

Printed and bound in China by by 1010 Printing International

www.theAA.com

Abbreviations used in the text

EH	English Heritage
HS	Historic Scotland
NT	National Trust
NTS	National Trust for Scotland
RSPB	Royal Society for the Protection of Birds

AA

NATIONAL PARKS OF BRITAIN

DARTMOOR • EXMOOR • NEW FOREST • SOUTH DOWNS • THE BROADS
PEAK DISTRICT • YORKSHIRE DALES • NORTH YORK MOORS • LAKE DISTRICT
NORTHUMBERLAND • PEMBROKESHIRE COAST • BRECON BEACONS
SNOWDONIA • LOCH LOMOND AND THE TROSSACHS • CAIRNGORMS

ROLY SMITH

FOREWORD BY
SIR CHRIS BONINGTON

CONTENTS

FOREWORD BY SIR CHRIS BONINGTON
A PRECIOUS HERITAGE 6

INTRODUCTION
YELLOWSTONE TO YORKSHIRE 8

CONCLUSION
JEWELS IN THE CROWN 232

MAPS

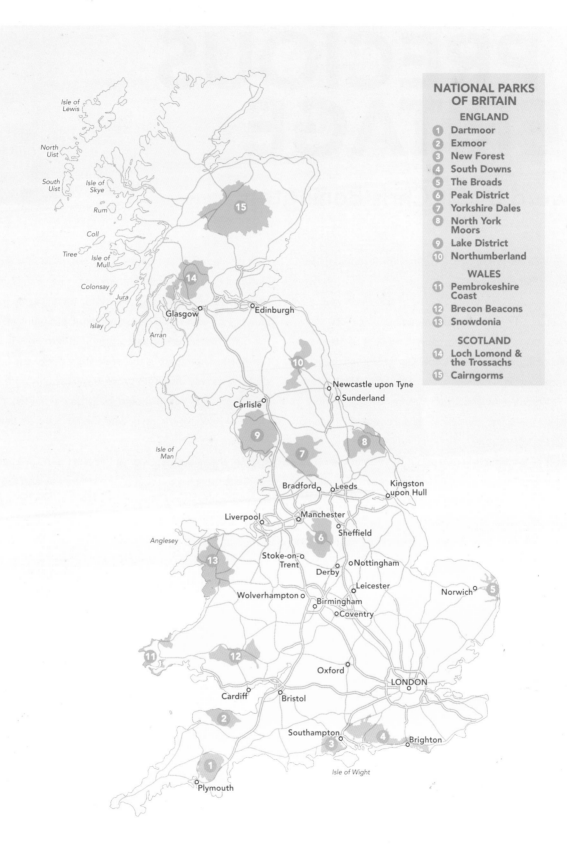

NATIONAL PARKS OF BRITAIN

ENGLAND
1. Dartmoor
2. Exmoor
3. New Forest
4. South Downs
5. The Broads
6. Peak District
7. Yorkshire Dales
8. North York Moors
9. Lake District
10. Northumberland

WALES
11. Pembrokeshire Coast
12. Brecon Beacons
13. Snowdonia

SCOTLAND
14. Loch Lomond & the Trossachs
15. Cairngorms

LEFT: Fallow deer doe in the New Forest

A PRECIOUS HERITAGE

Foreword by Sir Chris Bonington

Honorary Life Vice President of the Council for National Parks and President (1992–2000)

I'll never forget as a 17-year-old lad, on one of my earliest adventures into the hills, the first breathtaking sight of the snow-capped peaks of Snowdonia from Capel Curig, after hitch-hiking up the A5 from London. The initial view of that majestic horseshoe of Lliwedd, Yr Wyddfa and Crib Goch is as fresh in my memory today as it was on that first mind-blowing encounter 60 years ago.

I didn't know it at the time, of course, but this was in the very year that Snowdonia became one of the first of Britain's national parks, and it is a tribute to the way that the Park Authority has managed this spectacular landscape that I still get the same thrill when I see the view today. Later I spent many happy hours exploring the crags of Tryfan, Cwm Idwal, the Llanberis Pass and the finest of them all, Clogwyn Du'r Arddu – or 'Cloggy', as it is affectionately known to climbers – on Snowdon.

I fell in love with mountains there and then, and although I have travelled to the ends of the earth since, and seen many other superb mountain landscapes, I have seen nothing more beautiful than our British hills, many of which are now thankfully protected as national parks. They represent the cream of our countryside and are a valuable constant in an ever-changing world, as important to the millions who visit them every year as to those who are unable to do so.

I am privileged to live on the northern edge of the Lake District National Park, and when I return from one of my climbing trips abroad, usually driving up the M6 or travelling by train, I never lose that sense of excited anticipation as I first glimpse the distant serrated skyline of the Southern Fells from near Carnforth. Then there is the dramatic sight of the Lune Gorge, cleaving its way through the western Howgills on the right (the northern half of which should really be part of the Yorkshire Dales National Park like the rest), with the Borrowdale Fells on the left.

For me, this is the gateway to the Northern Lakes and my home. I can even forgive the roar of the motorway and the clatter of the iron-clad railway. Then to the left, or west, an ever-changing panorama of fells opens up – the Eastern Fells, High Street, the Dodds and, coming closer to Penrith, Saddleback (Blencathra) in all its glory, quickly followed by Carrock, with an Iron Age hill-fort crowning its summit. Getting closer to home is my beloved, gentle High Pike, up whose slopes I have walked so many times in the last 40 years. I love these fells with a passion because I have come to know them so well; but each one of our national parks has its own special and unique beauty.

No one knows these landscapes better than my good friend Roly Smith, who has explored them all and knows them as well as anyone. So it gives me great pleasure to write this foreword to this splendid book, which is a worthy celebration of the best of British landscapes – our precious heritage of the national parks.

RIGHT: Cadair Idris, Snowdonia

YELLOWSTONE TO YORKSHIRE

National parks have been described, with some justification, as the best idea America ever had. It can be argued, however, that there are several claimants to the idea – and the earliest was actually an Englishman.

An insignificant 7,549ft (2,300m) tree-covered mountain where the Firehole and Gibbon rivers merge to create the Madison in Yellowstone National Park, Montana, has the name National Park Mountain. This unusual appellation came about in September 1870 when a young Helena lawyer and newspaper correspondent, Cornelius Hedges, sat in the shadow of a campfire and suggested that the wonderland that is Yellowstone should be designated a national park.

Hedges served as a member of the Washburn-Doane expedition, charged with surveying the Yellowstone area and reporting back on some of the fantastical stories about the region. Mountain men like Jim Bridger and John Colter had come back from Yellowstone with extraordinary tales of hot springs and geysers, but they were simply not believed. As they sat around the campfire, the members of the expedition discussed earnestly how the obvious real estate and mineral resources of the area could best be exploited. But Hedges disagreed. There should be no private ownership of Yellowstone, he said. It should be a great national park for all people to enjoy forever.

Hedges' words struck a chord with the other members of the expedition. They had been overawed by the natural splendours they had seen, which bore out everything the old trappers had reported. Particularly affected was Nathaniel Langford, a local businessman, who campaigned vigorously to realise the dream. In 1872, Yellowstone became the first national park in the world when it was 'dedicated and set apart as a public park or pleasuring ground for the benefit and enjoyment of the people'. Although this incident is often quoted as the birth of the global national park movement, it was actually the painter of American Indians and diarist George Catlin who first came up with the idea of a Yellowstone National Park, in 1833. In a letter published in the New York *Daily Commercial Advertiser*, he recommended the creation of a 'nation's park' for the great herds of bison that roamed the northern plains at the confluence of the Yellowstone River with the upper Missouri.

'A NATIONAL PROPERTY'

More than 20 years before Catlin's vision, William Wordsworth (1770–1850), the celebrated English Lakeland Romantic poet, put the idea of a national park into words. In the concluding paragraphs of his *Guide to the Lakes* of 1810, he expressed the hope that landowners would join him in his wish 'to preserve the native beauty of this delightful district'.

He feared that the new owners, or 'gentry' as he called them, from the cities would 'erect new mansions out of the ruins of the ancient cottages', and hoped that 'a better taste should prevail' and that they would go down the 'path of simplicity and beauty… their humble predecessors have moved'. He even foretold the need for planning, because these nouveau riche landowners 'cannot be expected to leave things to themselves'. Finally, he famously suggested his beloved Lake District might be 'a sort of national property, in which every man has a right and interest who has an eye to perceive and a heart to enjoy'.

LEFT: Robin Hood's Bay, where the North York Moors meet the sea

But with the imminent arrival of the railway, he later qualified this far-sighted and democratically inclusive vision with the fear that the landscape would be destroyed if 'artisans, labourers and the humbler class of shopkeepers' were allowed to invade his precious fells. One wonders what he might think of today's traffic queues streaming off the motorway towards Windermere. Although they had been talked about for a hundred years, the idea of setting aside national parks like the American model in such a small, overcrowded island as Britain hardly seemed a possibility. With so little real wilderness, such a large population

and so much multiple land use, British national parks were always going to be a compromise. But when the promised 'land fit for heroes' failed to materialise after the carnage of World War I, agitation began again in the 1930s to get something done. By this time a series of Parliamentary bills, dating back half a century to James Bryce's in 1884, had proposed national parks for Britain, but all had failed at the last hurdle.

One of the key events that put the campaign on the front pages was the 1932 Mass Trespass onto Kinder Scout, the highest point

ABOVE: View over Wast Water towards Yewbarrow in the Lake District National Park

of the Peak District. It was a politically motivated event, which was as much about the right to roam as the creation of national parks, but they were certainly on the agenda. More than 400 ramblers gathered for the well-publicised trespass at Hayfield on 24 April (see panel, page 12). The resulting imprisonment of five young ramblers, who were merely exercising their right to roam, significantly raised public awareness of the rambling movement. Subsequent access rallies in the Peak District witnessed crowds of up to 10,000 pressing equally for the creation of national parks and the right to roam, and other mass trespasses followed.

THE DOWER BLUEPRINT

The start of the British national park 'adventure' can be traced to the dark final days of World War II, when the architect, town planner and rambler John Dower, Drafting Secretary of the Standing Committee on National Parks, joined Lord Reith's Ministry of Town and Country Planning in Whitehall. Between 1943 and 1945, Dower wrote his famous White Paper on national parks in England and Wales, which laid down the blueprint for the British parks. It was finally realised by the post-war Labour Government's groundbreaking National Parks

and Access to the Countryside Act in 1949. Dower's report was published on 12 April 1945, and it was he who came up with the classic definition of a British national park:

A national park may be defined, in application to Great Britain, as an extensive area of beautiful and relatively wild country in which, for the nation's benefit and by appropriate national decision and action:
• the characteristic landscape beauty is strictly preserved
• access and facilities for public open-air enjoyment are amply provided
• wildlife and buildings and places of architectural and historic interest are suitably protected, while
• established farming use is effectively maintained.

Dower proposed the creation of an initial 10 national parks in England and Wales. His remit did not extend to Scotland, where Sir Douglas Ramsay and mountaineer Bill Murray were

simultaneously preparing a report proposing the following areas as national parks: Loch Lomond and the Trossachs; the Cairngorms; Ben Nevis, Glen Coe and the Black Mount; Glen Affric, Glen Cannich and Strath Farrer; Torridon, Loch Maree and Loch Broom. Of these, Loch Lomond and the Trossachs and the Cairngorms eventually became Scotland's first national parks after the creation of the Scottish Parliament in 1999.

Dower's English and Welsh 'A list' included the Lake District, Snowdonia, Dartmoor, the Peak District (including Dovedale), the Pembrokeshire Coast, the Cornish Coast (selected parts), Craven Pennines (Wharfe, Aire and Ribble valleys), Brecon Beacons and Black Mountains, Exmoor (including the North Devon coast), and the Roman Wall. Of these, only the Cornish Coast is not a national park today.

Of Dower's second-tier, or reserve list, only the Broads, the North York Moors and, the latest addition in 2010, the South

FORGIVE US OUR TRESPASSERS

The Kinder Scout Mass Trespass of 24 April 1932 has been described as the most crucial event in the 100-year battle for the freedom to roam on Britain's mountains and moorlands.

Just 75 years ago, the highest and wildest moorlands of the Peak District remained frustratingly out of bounds to the growing army of walkers from the surrounding cities, and jealously guarded by gamekeepers for their grouse-shooting masters.

On that sunny Sunday morning, about 400 ramblers set off from Hayfield on the western side of

Kinder to trespass deliberately on what was then the Peak's 'forbidden mountain'. When they stepped off the path, a line of gamekeepers met them and a few undistinguished scuffles followed. A 'victory meeting' was held near Ashop Head and then the trespassers marched back to Hayfield where police arrested five people who were charged with public order offences such as riotous assembly.

At their trial at Derby Assizes, four of the five young defendants received prison sentences of between two and six months. Ironically, it was the severity of

the sentences which was to unite the ramblers' cause. The Kinder Scout Mass Trespass undoubtedly brought the access issue to a head, and acted as an important catalyst to the whole campaign for national parks and access to the countryside, which eventually led to legislation in 1949 (see page 15).

In 2011, Hayfield Parish Council announced plans for a £100,000 Trespass Heritage Centre in the village from where the trespassers set off. It will be housed in the former village lock-up in which the arrested trespassers were first held.

TOP, *LEFT TO RIGHT: John Dower; Tom Tomlinson, the first Peak warden, in around 1970; 1932 Mass Trespass onto Kinder Scout*

RIGHT: *View of Great Gable from Castle Crag, in the Lake District*

Downs, have become fully fledged national parks. The smooth slopes of the southern Howgills and the rugged Swaledale Pennines became part of the Yorkshire Dales National Park when it was designated in 1954, and the peaty summits of the northeast Cheviots were included in the Northumberland National Park, along with Hadrian's Wall, in 1956.

When he wrote his seminal report, John Dower was a sick man. He had been invalided out of the Army in 1940 suffering from the advanced stages, albeit undiagnosed, of terminal tuberculosis. Dower never saw the fruits of his inspiration. He died of TB just two years later, shortly after the committee chaired by Sir Arthur Hobhouse, of which he was also a member, had recommended the setting up of 12 national parks (including the South Downs and the Broads) in 1947. At last the tide had turned, and national parks in Britain became a real possibility.

'A PEOPLE'S CHARTER'

The 1949 National Parks and Access to the Countryside Act, passed on 16 December, proposed the setting up of a National Parks Commission to preserve and enhance the natural beauty of England and Wales, particularly in national parks or as Areas of Outstanding Natural Beauty, and encourage the provision of facilities for their enjoyment. The Act also proposed the creation of long-distance paths for use on foot or on horseback; Areas of Outstanding Natural Beauty; and, where necessary, access agreements with landowners to allow the public free access to open country (or access orders, where agreement could not

be reached). Ramblers would have to wait for another 50 years before the passing of the Countryside and Rights of Way Act in 2000 finally gave them their holy grail of the right to roam on mountain and moorland, and 16 years before the creation of the first long-distance footpath – Tom Stephenson's 250-mile (400km) Pennine Way (see panel, page 16).

It was perhaps significant that it was the Peak District, the scene of the access battle of the 1930s, that became the first British national park on 17 April 1951, shortly followed by William Wordsworth's 'national property' of the Lake District. Eight others – Snowdonia, Dartmoor, the Pembrokeshire Coast, the North York Moors, the Yorkshire Dales, Exmoor, Northumberland and the Brecon Beacons – followed at regular intervals throughout the 1950s. All the first national parks were in Dower's 'beautiful and relatively wild country', in the more mountainous, upland parts of England and Wales. They ranged from the craggy heights of the Lake District and Snowdonia to the vast, desolate moorlands of Dartmoor and Exmoor in the southwest and the Pennines and the sun-kissed cliffs of Pembrokeshire.

There were no national parks in the lowlands until the deceptively natural but actually man-made fens of the Norfolk and Suffolk Broads joined the family in 1989. Currently, 10 per cent of the area of England and Wales falls within national parks, and their designation is the responsibility of Natural England (the governmental successor to the National Parks Commission, the Countryside Commission and the Countryside Agency) and the

LEFT: Whitesands Bay with Ramsey Island in the distance, part of the Pembrokeshire Coast National Park

TOP, LEFT TO RIGHT: The Cambrian Mountains; Bedruthan Steps, near Newquay in north Cornwall

THE PENNINE WAY

Like the first national park, the idea for Britain's first long-distance footpath (national trail) came from the United States of America.

In 1935, access campaigner and journalist Tom Stephenson was working as the open-air correspondent for the **Daily Herald** newspaper. He received a letter from two American girls who were visiting on a walking holiday and wondered if there was anything similar in Britain to the American Appalachian Trail.

At the time, of course, there wasn't, but the letter set Stephenson thinking and he published his thoughts about a possible 'Long Green Trail' – a Pennine Way from the Peak to the Cheviots – in the **Herald**.

'This need be no Euclidean line,' he wrote, 'but a meandering way deviating as needs be to include the best of that long range of moor and fell; no concrete or asphalt track, but just a faint line on the Ordnance Maps which the feet of grateful pilgrims would, with the passing years, engrave on the face of the land'.

It was to take another 30 years before Tom Stephenson's dream came to fruition. Stephenson admitted later that his hidden agenda for the Pennine Way was to open up the then-forbidden moorlands of the Pennines to walkers.

The 250-mile (400km) Pennine Way remains one of Britain's toughest national trails. Because of its popularity with long-distance walkers, it has been paved in some places, using recycled slabs from derelict cotton mills.

TOP: *Thurne Mill, in the Broads*

Countryside Council for Wales. North of the Border, things took a little longer, but with the creation of the Scottish Parliament in 1999, the devolved government acted quickly through Scottish Natural Heritage to designate the popular honeypots of Loch Lomond and the Trossachs and the semi-arctic Cairngorms as Scotland's first national parks in 2002 and 2003 respectively. The paradoxically ancient New Forest joined the clan in 2005. The last member of the national parks family was the South Downs, first proposed as a national park by Sir Arthur Hobhouse in 1947, and eventually designated by the Countryside Agency in 2002. After prolonged arguments over its boundaries, in particular the inclusion of the Western Weald, the South Downs finally became Britain's 15th national park in April 2011, some 60 years after it was first proposed. Consultations and a public inquiry over proposed extensions to the Lake District and Yorkshire Dales national parks, which would join the two north of Sedbergh, took place in 2013. These changes, if ratified, would increase the area of the Yorkshire Dales National Park by nearly a quarter (24 per cent, or 162 square miles) and the Lake District by three per cent (28 square miles). But as this book went to press, no decision had been taken by the Secretary of State for the Environment.

VALUE OF THE PARKS

The national parks of Britain currently receive over 150 million day visits every year, and an awareness survey of the English and Welsh parks undertaken in 2007 showed that nine out of ten people interviewed knew what they were and felt they were important and, perhaps significantly, that every child should experience a national park as part of their education.

Half of all adults interviewed had visited several national parks and had visited one once or more often that year. The most

ABOVE: Reindeer in the Cairngorms

popular of the recently visited parks were the Lake District, the Peak District and the New Forest, and the least visited were Northumberland, the Pembrokeshire Coast, Exmoor, the Broads and the Brecon Beacons.

The economic value of the national parks has only recently begun to be realised. A major research project commissioned by the Council for National Parks in 2006 looked at the economic impact of the Yorkshire Dales, North York Moors and Peak District national parks on the Yorkshire and Humber region. The project estimated that sales by businesses in the parks were worth £1.8 billion annually and supported over 34,000 jobs, and that the spending by park visitors amounted to £400 million annually within the parks and a further £260 million elsewhere in the region, supporting another 12,000 jobs. With 'knock-on' effects, the total impact of this £660 million expenditure on the region's output was estimated to be almost £1 billion.

A similar exercise in the three Welsh parks in the same year concluded that they produced a total income of £177 million and supported nearly 12,000 jobs, generating £205 million of the gross domestic product of Wales. And a 2010 survey of the economic and social health of the Cairngorms National Park showed that there had been an increase in population and that between 2003 and 2007, the park had attracted 1,000 new residents. There was also a 13 per cent increase in the number of businesses operating in the park since designation, a decrease in unemployment, and a reduction in the seasonality of jobs, creating more steady employment.

The growing economy of the Cairngorms National Park is currently worth £398 million per year, with tourism accounting for just under a third (£115 million) of that amount. This relatively recent realisation of the economic worth of the national parks takes us full circle to the views of the members of the Washburn-Doane expedition in Yellowstone 140 years ago.

Although some British parks, such as the Peak District and the Yorkshire Dales, are still valued for their mineral wealth by quarrymen, their greatest asset will always be their wild beauty and the breathing space they provide for millions of visitors, for this and future generations.

TOP: The red kite was brought back from extinction in the Cambrian Mountains of mid Wales, site of a proposed national park

NATIONAL PARKS OF BRITAIN

	Designated	Area in square miles (sq km)	Population	Annual day visits (millions)
Peak District	1951	555 (1,437)	38,100	19.0
Lake District	1951	885 (2,292)	42,200	15.2
Snowdonia	1951	840 (2,176)	25,480	10.4
Dartmoor	1951	368 (954)	34,000	3.3
Pembrokeshire Coast	1952	240 (621)	22,800	13.5
North York Moors	1952	554 (1,434)	25,000	9.0
Yorkshire Dales	1954	683 (1,769)	19,650	12.6
Exmoor	1954	267 (694)	10,600	2.0
Northumberland	1956	404 (1,048)	2,200	2.4
Brecon Beacons	1957	518 (1,344)	32,000	4.3
The Broads	1989	117 (305)	5,500	7.2
Loch Lomond & the Trossachs	2002	720 (1,864)	15,600	4.0
Cairngorms	2003	1,748 (4,528)	17,000	3.0
New Forest	2005	220 (570)	34,400	13.5
South Downs	2010	636 (1,648)	107,900	39.0

TOP TEN NATIONAL TRAILS
❶ Pennine Way
❷ South West Coast Path
❸ Pembrokeshire Coast Path
❹ Offa's Dyke Path
❺ Cotswold Way
❻ The Ridgeway
❼ West Highland Way
❽ South Downs Way
❾ Cleveland Way
❿ Southern Upland Way

ABOVE, LEFT TO RIGHT: Offa's Dyke Path on the Welsh/English border; signpost on the Pennine Way national trail

DARTMOOR

Over the centuries, man… has left his traces on our wild uplands, and these age-old survivals are an essential part of their value and interest. The little prehistoric hut circles, the rings of standing stones, the wavering marks of the ox plough, the ruins of the long-gone tinners' huts and workings – these can be sought out in the lonely places, and they speak to us and fire our imagination and sense of history. Lady Sylvia Sayer (1904–2000), *Wild Country* (1971)

A GRANITE FIST

At first sight, the tor-topped, sweeping sepia moorland expanses of Dartmoor, where fleeting shadows of clouds constantly change both the light and the mood of the moors, appear to bear out its well-worn epithet as the last wilderness of southern Britain. It doesn't seem possible that anything could live on this bleak expanse of rough moor grass and heather, apart from the occasional drift of shock-headed ponies, or flocks of hardy moorland sheep.

But look a little closer and you will see plenty of evidence of life. Dartmoor's apparently primeval landscape is in fact one of Britain's finest examples of what archaeologists call a palimpsest – a landscape on which layer upon layer of human activity has left its mark.

Perhaps the epitome of the Dartmoor palimpsest is the moorland as seen from the col between Hameldown and Hookney Tor, northwest of Widecombe-in-the-Moor.

LEFT: The North Teign River, near Chagford

In the foreground, enclosed by a stone wall, lies Grimspound, probably the most famous and complete Bronze Age settlement in England. The remains of round houses are outlined in the granite moorstone of their walls, and stand out clearly through the purple heather. On the ridge above, a line of cairns or barrows acted as both landscape features and burial places for these Dartmoor residents of some 4,000 years ago.

Further down the valley of the West Webburn there are more hut circles, and on Challacombe Down are the remains of a prehistoric stone row, which marches up its northern flank above the later opencast tin workings.

On the slopes above the enclosures of the late 16th-century Headland Warren Farm, the extensive remains of tin working can be seen: spoil heaps and deep, ravine-like gullies, which cut into the surface of the moor. In the valley of the West Webburn, parallel ridges show where medieval miners had 'streamed' for alluvial tin.

ABOVE: *The remains of the Bronze Age settlement at Grimspound*

Extensive remains of tin working and processing can be found throughout central Dartmoor. Around the fringes, away from the granite mass, other minerals such as copper, lead and silver were exploited. The engine house of the silver and lead mine of Wheal Betsy, near Mary Tavy, is the most complete example of its kind on Dartmoor.

The Devonport Leat, constructed in the 1790s, took pure water from Dartmoor to Devonport, in Plymouth, to supply the growing population of the port. The many miles of leats (artificial water channels), which carried water to mills and mines to drive waterwheels, still wind round the hillsides.

The name of Headland Warren is a clue to yet another occupation on Dartmoor – this time dating from the Middle Ages. Rabbits, which were introduced into Britain by the Normans for their meat, were bred in artificial warrens, and Headland Warren, created at the beginning of the 18th century, was one of the biggest. Cigar-shaped mounds known as 'pillow mounds' were also constructed to encourage the rabbits to burrow and breed. The Warren House Inn on the B3212 northeast of the town of Postbridge serves as a reminder of this historic activity.

Over on the slopes of Challacombe Down, distinct parallel lines of terraces can be seen extending along the hillside. These are the remains of medieval strip lynchets, created by the build-up of oxen-ploughed soil against the boundaries of the ancient fields. Astonishing as it may seem today, cereal crops were grown here.

DARTMOOR PONIES

One extremely familiar aspect of Dartmoor's varied wildlife is the sturdy ponies that freely graze the open moorland.

It is fitting, therefore, that an outline of a prancing pony was chosen to be the logo of the Dartmoor National Park. These ponies epitomise the wild, free nature of the park. Yet they are all owned by someone, and carry distinctive ear or tail marks denoting ownership. Although unbroken, they are carefully managed to see that they remain healthy.

First mentioned in 11th-century writings, the ponies are thought to have descended from Bronze Age stock and were used by farmers to pull carts and as pack animals.

Today, the 3,000 or so ponies on the moor (about 12 hands or 4ft/1.2m high and mostly brown or bay in colour) are collected annually in autumn 'drifts'. Here they are rounded up and many are sold as riding ponies for children because they are noted for their friendly disposition.

ABOVE: All the ponies roaming free in Dartmoor National Park are owned by farmers who have grazing rights

TOP: The clapper bridge at Postbridge, built with slabs of granite

ABOVE, LEFT TO RIGHT: Cattle and a solitary hawthorn tree, near Hay Tor

TOP SIGHTS

1. *Buckfast Abbey, Buckfast:* abbey rebuilt in the early 20th century.

2. *Castle Drogo (NT), Drewsteignton:* property designed by Edwin Lutyens; completed in 1931.

3. *Dartmoor National Park High Moorland Visitor Centre, Princetown:* learn all there is to know about the national park.

4. *House of Marbles, Teign Valley Glassworks, Bovey Tracey:* glass marbles, traditional toys and games made in the former pottery.

5. *Lydford Gorge (NT), near Okehampton:* a 98ft (30m) waterfall and trails through oak woodland.

6. *Museum of Dartmoor Life, Okehampton:* find out how people have lived on Dartmoor over the last 100 years.

7. *Okehampton Castle (EH), Okehampton:* the largest castle in Devon.

8. *St Michael's Church, Brent Tor, near North Brentor:* 13th-century church that may have been used as a beacon.

The ancient woodlands of the national park, such as Wistman's Wood, in the valley of the West Dart above Two Bridges, are rare examples of ancient upland English oakwoods.

The enchanted, fairy-tale qualities of these woods have attracted much descriptive prose, and their survival is probably due to the fact that they somehow have managed to grow straight out of the moss-covered rock 'clitter', which has effectively protected them from the nibbling teeth of grazing sheep.

The draping lichens and mosses that grow in these woodlands not only indicate a very clean atmosphere but they are also rare in Britain, and the woodlands are protected as SSSIs (Sites of Special Scientific Interest).

The wreaths and trails of lichens and ferns that grow from the weirdly contorted and stunted branches evoke the atmosphere of an Arthur Rackham illustrated fairy tale, and you almost expect to see a pixie appearing from between the trees.

More likely is a sighting of a pied flycatcher, a mid-April migrant from Africa that only colonised these oak woodlands in the 1950s. Other birdlife includes tree pipits and greater spotted woodpeckers.

THE GRAND TORS

The key to the remarkable preservation of Dartmoor's historic and prehistoric features lies in its geology. Dartmoor is the last and largest 'knuckle' in a gigantic granite subterranean fist, which extends across the West Country outcropping from Dartmoor through Bodmin Moor and Land's End to the Scilly Isles. About 280 million years ago, molten granite forced its way up through the younger sedimentary rocks above – in a formation known to geologists as a batholith – and slowly cooled and revealed through erosion the abrasive, distinctive, grey granite bosses that characterise the area we see today.

Most of Dartmoor's prehistoric monuments, from the stone circles to the network of territorial boundaries known as reaves (see panel, page 30), are made from this enduring stone. But the most prominent physical landmarks of Dartmoor today are the tors, those great, organic masses of granite that top many of the hills and act as a magnet for visitors and a navigational tool for walkers.

There has been much discussion about how the tors were formed, but the consensus appears to be that they are the weathered remains of more resistant underlying granite which, once exposed by erosion, has withstood Dartmoor's ice, wind and rain better than the surrounding rocks. They now remain, each quite different and highly individual sculptures and symbols of Dartmoor's permanence and its fiery birth.

Impressive examples include the massive elephant's-hide lump of Haytor, near Bovey Tracey; the natural 'Andy Cap' rock sculpture of Bowerman's Nose on Hayne Down above Manaton; Crockern Tor near Two Bridges, where the medieval tin miners held their Stannary parliament; and the church-topped basaltic outcrop of Brent Tor, near North Brentor in the far west of the national park.

Many tors, such as Vixen Tor on the western edge of the moor near Merrivale (to which there is currently no right of access), have myths attached to them. This towering, 100ft high (30m)

LEFT: Buckfast Abbey
TOP: Wistman's Wood, west of Postbridge

granite outcrop was said to be the home of a wicked witch known as Vixana, after whom the tor was probably named. She tempted travellers into the notorious bog below the tor by conjuring up a thick mist, which lured them from the safe path and into the treacherous arms of the marsh. With a wild, unearthly cackle, Vixana would then consume her unfortunate victims.

One day, however, the mist enveloped a traveller carrying a magic ring, which allowed him to see through the haze and become invisible if he wished. Using the powers of this ring,

he safely negotiated the bog. On hearing Vixana's wicked laugh from the top of the tor, he became invisible and crept up behind her, pushing her over to meet her death below.

One of Brent Tor's many legends is that the church that crowns it was built by the Archangel Michael, but every night after he had started work on the church the Devil would come and tear it down. Eventually Michael waited to see who was removing the stones. Seeing the Devil at work, he threw a boulder, which struck Old Nick on the head – and the Evil One never returned.

TOP: Sunrise from Crockern Tor at the heart of the park

A more grisly folktale of Dartmoor relates to Childe's Tomb, near Foxtor Mires on the southern moor. Marking the spot today is a worn, medieval waymarker cross, which stands on a prehistoric burial mound or cist. The story goes that the cross marks the spot where Childe, a local hunter, was separated from his companions on a wild winter's day while out riding, and eventually became hopelessly lost in a violent blizzard. Overcome by the cold, Childe killed his horse and crawled inside its corpse to escape the biting wind and snow. But his blood-soaked clothes soon froze and when he was found days later –

perhaps by monks from nearby Tavistock – he had died inside his ghastly shelter. Another version of the tale dates back to Saxon times, claiming that the hunter was a *cild*, or leader.

One of the best known Dartmoor legends is concerned with the writings of Sir Arthur Conan Doyle (1859–1930) and his famous fictional character, the detective Sherlock Holmes. In *The Hound of the Baskervilles*, first serialised in *The Strand* magazine in 1901, Conan Doyle's description of Dartmoor, 'so vast, and so barren, and so mysterious', has seldom been bettered.

His fearsome description of the Great Grimpen Mire is believed to have been inspired by Foxtor Mires in the heart of the moor, which probably gave rise to the largely unfounded evil reputation of Dartmoor's quaking bogs. But it was Holmes's loyal lieutenant, Dr Watson, who perhaps best encapsulated the moor's elemental sense of brooding history:

> *On all sides of you as you walk are the houses of these forgotten folk, with their graves and the large monoliths which are supposed to mark their temples. As you look at their grey stone huts against the scarred hillsides you leave your own age behind you, and if you were to see a skin-clad, hairy man crawl out from the low door, you would feel that his presence there was more natural than your own.*

A LONG HISTORY

Dartmoor takes its name from being the birthplace of the mighty River Dart, and the East and West Dart meet at Dartmeet in the centre of the moor, combining to flow south, then swinging east through the pleasant abbey town of Buckfastleigh. From Dartmoor, the only river heading north to the Bristol Channel is the River Taw, fed by the West and East Okement rivers. Dartmeet illustrates the complete history of river crossings on Dartmoor – everything from stepping stones to a clapper bridge

and an arched road bridge dating from 1792. Other famous clapper bridges – flat slabs of rock placed between piers or banks – can be seen at Postbridge and Teignhead, constructed from medieval times through to the 19th century.

In medieval times, Dartmoor was designated as a royal hunting forest, but at that time the word forest did not necessarily mean wooded. Most of the extensive woodland that formed after the last Ice Age was cleared by neolithic times, and the only remains of the wildwood on the open moor today are the oak woodlands of Wistman's Wood on the slopes of the West Dart near Two Bridges (see panel, page 27), Black-a-Tor Copse in the West Okement valley, and Piles Copse on the Erme above Harford.

Dartmoor's weather can be harsh and the central parts of the moor have an annual rainfall average of 66in (1.69m). Nevertheless, it supports an exceptional variety of wildlife and its natural heritage is internationally important. Sheep and ponies (see panel, page 24) graze the moor, joined by cattle in the summer months. The mewing cry of the buzzard and the harsh croak of the raven can often be heard on a moorland ramble, and in the shelter of the wooded valleys badger, fox and even the shy otter still flourish. A fine summer's day will reward the walker with the sound of the skylark's song and perhaps the sight of a rare fritillary butterfly.

TOP: Ancient cultivation terraces

You can still see where offenders against the penal system were imprisoned in the four-square block of Lydford Castle. A motte-and-bailey construction was built by the Norman conquerors at Okehampton, followed by a more substantial stone-built structure.

Quarrying began in the early part of the 19th century when granite was extracted from the old quarries near Haytor to be used for Nelson's Column, London Bridge (now in Arizona), Holborn Viaduct and New Scotland Yard in London. The stone sets of the earliest horsedrawn tramway, which carried the stone down to Teignmouth for shipping, can still be seen in the velvety grass on Haytor Down.

Dartmoor's granite has provided building stone for thousands of years and it dominates the built landscape; prehistoric houses and ceremonial monuments, medieval farmhouses and later cottages, churches, castles and mine buildings have all been constructed from 'moorstone', removed from the moor's surface.

Enormous 'moonscape' quarries and spoilheaps can be seen around Lee Moor in the southwestern corner of the national park. The dazzlingly white clay – a weathered form of granite known as kaolin – has been quarried for more than 150 years and was originally used in the making of porcelain, but today its main use is for making paper.

ABOVE, LEFT TO RIGHT: The ruins of Wheal Betsy mine; Lustleigh village; stepping stones across the East Dart at Dartmeet

TOP: Scorhill stone circle near Okehampton – only about half of the original 70-odd stones remain

LETTERBOXING

During the 19th and early 20th centuries, encouraged by guidebooks such as William Crossing's Guide to Dartmoor, more people started to visit the wilder parts of Dartmoor. One of these was the remote Cranmere Pool, located near the watershed of the Dart, Tor and Oakmeet rivers in the centre of the northern moor.

In 1854, local guide James Perrott of Chagford built a cairn at the pool and left a glass jar and visiting book so that visitors to Cranmere Pool could leave their cards or sign the book. Others followed at Taw Marsh, Ducks Pool and Fur Tor, starting off a craze, and now there are more than 100 of these 'letterboxes' scattered over the moor.

Letterboxing is now a semi-organised 'sport' administered by the Dartmoor 100 Club, and the Dartmoor National Park Authority has published a code of practice that aims to regulate letterbox owners and letterboxers seeking out their objectives.

ABOVE: St Peter's Church, Buckland in the Moor

THE ARRIVAL OF TOURISM

Tourists first started to visit Dartmoor in large numbers after the Railway Age dawned. Between 1806 and 1809, Thomas Tyrwhitt (1762–1833), who had unsuccessfully attempted to make large-scale agricultural improvements on the moor in the previous century, constructed Dartmoor Prison at Princetown for French prisoners of war: it was converted into Britain's most infamous civil prison in 1850. Tyrwhitt then set up a horsedrawn tramway to link his new town at Princetown, first with nearby quarries and by 1827 with Plymouth. It was converted to steam power in 1877 and enabled tourists to visit the moor. The Exeter–Plymouth line, running down the eastern and southern fringes of the moor, and the Exeter to Plymouth railway, passing through Okehampton and Tavistock, provided further points of access to Dartmoor.

The British military started using Dartmoor as a training area in 1873 and still occupy around 14 per cent (33,340 acres/13,492ha) of the park's northern moor, most of which is leased from the Duchy of Cornwall. The Ministry of Defence training area on northern Dartmoor comprises the Okehampton, Merrivale and Willsworthy ranges. The public has access to these moorland areas except when the ranges are in use for live firing. A series of red and white posts with warning notices marks the boundaries of these ranges. Firing programmes are published in information centres and local newspapers.

Dartmoor's eight reservoirs, including Fernworthy, Burrator, Venford and Meldon, were built to realise the water-gathering potential of the area and provide fresh water to the surrounding towns and cities. Six of the eight reservoirs had been built before the designation of the national park, and although entirely unnatural, attract large numbers of visitors. During the 20th century, the fast-expanding populations of surrounding towns increasingly started to drive to Dartmoor for their recreation, and the Dartmoor National Park was finally designated in 1951.

Dartmoor was the fourth area in Britain to be designated a national park, and it now has around 3.3 million visitors every year, most of whom come from the nearby towns of Plymouth and Torbay. It provides a vital 'lung', a place to get away from it all and savour Dartmoor's special sense of wilderness.

TOP: Dartmoor Prison at Princetown

EXMOOR

The Exmoor immortalised by R. D. Blackmore in his romantic novel *Lorna Doone* (1869) and Henry Williamson in his rural classic *Tarka the Otter* (1927) is a landscape of plunging coombs, deep wooded valleys, and crystal-clear streams, watched over by brooding moorland.

'EX-MOOR'

Exmoor is one of the smallest, most intimate and least visited of the national parks. Designated in 1954 as the eighth in the series, the park's central and eastern parts lie in Somerset, and its northern and western fringes in Devon.

During the 1960s and 1970s, Exmoor was also one of the most threatened of the national parks as agricultural 'improvements' were allowed to nibble away at its last remaining areas of moorland. One cynical commentator was even prompted to call it 'Ex-moor', as the amount of true moorland dwindled from about a third of the 267 square mile (694sq km) area that was designated to be the national park to a fragmented quarter of the total area today.

The Portchester Report of 1977 highlighted the threat to the moorland and recommended that where it constituted an important element of the national park's landscape, it should be 'conserved so far as possible for all time'. Within the shrinking moorland area, the report urged that there should be 'the strongest possible presumption against agricultural conversion'.

Since those bad old days, the National Park Authority, together with the National Trust (which owns and protects about a tenth of the park), has largely halted the large-scale decimation of Exmoor. So it is still possible to wander over areas like The Chains, which rise to nearly 1,600ft (487m), or the highest point of Dunkery Beacon at 1,704ft (519m), and feel what the Parliamentary Commissioners of 1651 described as 'A mountenous and cold ground much be-Clouded with thick Foggs and Mists… overgrown with heath, and yielding but a poor kind of turf.'

Today, among the best places to see what Exmoor once looked like are the commons, such as those at Brendon, Withypool, Dunkery Hill and Wilmersham. These are the unreclaimed parts of medieval manors, where the local lords allowed farmers to use the commons for the grazing of their animals. But even here, as wild as it may seem, man has influenced the landscape.

The wonderful vista of blooming heather, especially magnificent in late August and early September in places such as Holdstone Down, Countisbury Common, Yenworthy Common, Porlock

LEFT: The view towards the Bristol Channel and the distant hills of Wales from Dunkery Beacon

Common and North Hill, along the coast, and at Anstey and Molland commons in the south of the park, is the creation of generations of grazing animals, and many years of careful land management by owners.

To give that superb display of heather – mainly ling, but mixed here and there with the deeper purple bell heather and splashes of the bright yellow western gorse – the heathland is systematically burned, known locally as 'swaling', during the winter and early spring when the risk of fire spreading is at its lowest. This clears the dead growth of the previous year and promotes the growth of fresh young shoots for the grazing animals, which nowadays are mainly sheep.

In late summer, when the heather is in bloom and alive with the buzzing of bees, you will often see rows of hives put out along the edges of the heath by beekeepers keen to obtain supplies of the delicious heather honey.

TOP: The cairn on the summit of Dunkery Beacon

ABOVE, LEFT TO RIGHT: Gorse; the park sign; heather in flower

EXMOOR PONIES

Shaggy-maned Exmoor ponies are reckoned to be the nearest thing Britain has to a wild horse. Similar ponies roamed the tundra shortly after the last Ice Age, and with their thick, waterproof coats they are well adapted to harsh weather conditions.

The normal colour is chestnut, with a white to grey muzzle and lighter hair around their eyelids. With their large jaws and thick lips, they can also eat very rough vegetation, even the spiny needles of gorse. In recent years they have found a new role as 'conservation grazers', keeping down unwanted scrub in nature reserves all over the country.

A few ponies still graze freely across the moor, and a gene pool of pure stock is maintained by the Exmoor Pony Society, using herds which are kept by the National Trust and National Park Authority.

TOP: Moorland at County Gate, with the East Lyn valley beyond

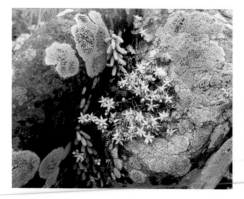

TOP, LEFT TO RIGHT: *Stonecrop at Porlock Weir; Heddon's Mouth; cliffs at Heddon's Mouth cove; view from the Valley of the Rocks*

ABOVE: *Looking across Porlock Bay from Hurlstone Point*

SWITCHBACK COAST

Apart from the moorland heights, the other place where you can still find wildest Exmoor is on the 30-mile (48km) stretch of coastline within the park, which includes some of the highest cliffs in England. This coast forms some spectacular stretches of the 630-mile (1,014km) South West Coast Path – Britain's longest national trail – and the switchback section between the northern terminus at the seaside resort of Minehead and Combe Martin in the west is as challenging as anywhere on the trail.

The north-facing cliffs of Hangman Hill, Duty Point and Foreland Point offer a far-reaching view across the Bristol Channel towards the distant blue hills of Preseli, South Wales, on the horizon. Meanwhile, the deep wooded cleaves of Heddon's Mouth, Woody Bay and the West and East Lyn valleys are beautiful at any time of the year, but perhaps especially in autumn.

Some of the highest cliffs are between Foreland and Porlock Weir, where they drop more than 1,200ft (365m) to the sea within a mile (1.6km). Here, at Exmoor's most northerly point, woodlands of crazily twisted and stunted oaks grow right down to the edge of the stony, pebbled beach. This rare juxtaposition of woodland and coast gives rise to unlikely neighbours, so you may see woodpeckers and jays mixing with fulmars and oystercatchers on the beach. And even shy deer from the woodland have been known to come down and beachcomb.

One of the reasons for this abundance of wildlife is that this section of coastline is virtually inaccessible to most visitors, the only point of access being at Glenthorne, where the road drops over 1,000ft (300m) from the A39 at County Gate. It is difficult and dangerous to walk along this boulder-strewn beach, especially without a thorough knowledge of the tides; it is very easy to become trapped under the cliffs by a rising tide.

Perhaps the most dramatic part of the coastline is the section between the spectacular dry canyon of the Valley of the Rocks near Lynton and Heddon's Mouth, where a dizzying alternative path – not for the inexperienced walker – passes the Hollow Brook falls, and the air is filled with the elemental cries of guillemots, kittiwakes and razorbills.

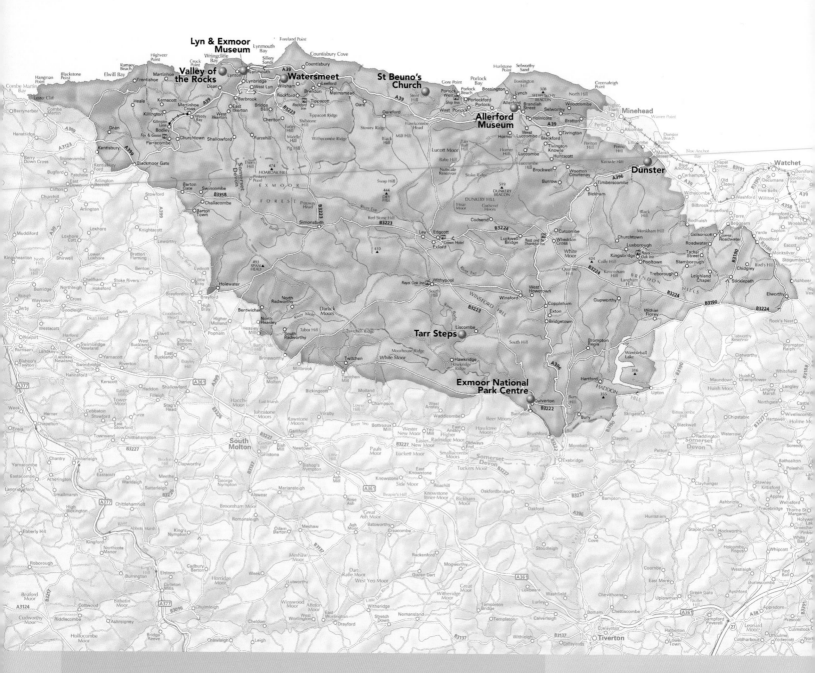

TOP SIGHTS

1. *Allerford Museum, Allerford:* rural life museum and photographic archive of West Somerset.

2. *Dunster:* castle (NT) and yarn market: turreted castle with terraced gardens and views of the Bristol Channel. Octagonal wooden yarn market in village below.

3. *Exmoor National Park Centre, Dulverton:* displays here include the heritage of Dulverton and an art gallery.

4. *Lyn and Exmoor Museum, Lynton:* stone cottage housing domestic bygones, displays and more.

5. *St Beuno's Church, Culbone, near Porlock:* reputedly the smallest church in England.

6. *Tarr Steps, near Simonsbath:* a classic prehistoric clapper bridge.

7. *Valley of the Rocks:* spectacular valley to the west of Lynton.

8. *Watersmeet (NT), near Lynmouth:* river gorge and ancient woodland, with waterfalls and walks. Tea room and shop in a former fishing lodge.

The aptly named Valley of the Rocks, near Lynton, seems strangely out of place in the gentle Exmoor scene. Here towering crags and a narrow, rocky ridge parallel the coast, rising up abruptly out of a velvety-green, dry valley, giving a fair impression of a Highland glen. Geologists believe that the Valley of the Rocks marks the original course of the East and West Lyn rivers. Erosion caused by the pounding waves of the Bristol Channel eventually cut off and captured the valley and its rivers, so they now flow out into the sea at Lynmouth, leaving the Valley of the Rocks literally high and dry.

As well as being a popular picnic site, the Valley of the Rocks is also inhabited by a herd of goats with distinctive black and white coats, often seen scampering nimbly along the rocky crests, and even invading local gardens. The highest crag on the ridge is known as Rugged Jack and, as so often is the case with unusual physical features in the West Country, it has its own legend attached to it.

The story goes that the name comes from the leader of a group of drunken revellers who were illicitly making merry on the Sabbath. The Devil, not wishing to miss out on such sacrilegious fun, couldn't wait to join in, but Jack and the others were so drunk they didn't recognise his satanic majesty. Not best pleased with this lack of respect, the Devil promptly turned the luckless merrymakers to stone. A similarly severe punishment was meted out to dancing maidens, who can be seen as stone circles throughout the country.

LEFT: Tarr Steps across the River Barle
TOP: Castle Rock, in the Valley of the Rocks, at sunset

ABOVE, LEFT TO RIGHT: Scabious; coast path signs; lichen-covered rock in the Valley of the Rocks

ON TARKA'S TRAIL

Henry Williamson's subtitle to his famous classic was *His Joyful Water-Life and Death in the Country of the Two Rivers*. The two rivers in Williamson's title could be the Exe and the Barle, Exmoor's major waterways, which rise high on the moor on the boggy, tumulus-topped area known as The Chains. Despite the fact that its source is less than 5 miles (8km) away from the Bristol Channel, the Exe perversely turns its back on the easy route. It swings east and then south to join the Barle below Dulverton and make the tortuous 50-mile (80km) journey across Devon to flow into the English Channel at Exeter on the south coast.

In his best-known book, based on his experiences when he lived in a 1s 6d (7.5p) a week cob-built cottage on the North Devon coast, Williamson describes Exmoor as: 'the high country of the winds, which are to the falcons and the hawks; clothed by whortleberry bushes and lichens and ferns and moss-enrobed trees in the goyals (moorland valleys), which are to the foxes, the badgers, and the red deer; served by rain clouds and drained by rock-littered streams, which are to the otters.'

Tarka is an Exmoor otter cub growing up with his mother and siblings. When hunters attack his home, he and his family flee and join up with another bevy of otters, but Tarka loses track of his family and has to fend for himself. Eventually, after being chased by otter hounds, he meets his end in an epic fight with the fearsome lead hound, Deadlock, who dies with him.

Williamson began working on a script for a film of his novel in 1974, but it was rejected as not suitable. Eventually, with a screenplay by fellow naturalist Gerald Durrell, filming for the movie went on unbeknown to him. Williamson died, bitterly disappointed, in August 1977, by an extraordinary coincidence on the same day on which the death of Tarka was being filmed. Narrated by Peter Ustinov, the film was released in 1979 and became a firm box-office favourite.

You can still follow the Tarka Trail, a 180-mile (289km) figure-of-eight long-distance walk centred on Barnstaple, to the west of the national park, which features various possible locations from the book. The northern section of the trail takes an easterly line over Exmoor to reach the sea and a stretch of the route makes use of the Tarka Line railway line. It is appropriately waymarked by the symbol of an otter's paw print.

DOONELAND

The other famous author associated with the moor is Richard Doddridge (R. D.) Blackmore, whose one-and-only novel, *Lorna Doone*, published in 1869, was subtitled *A Romance of Exmoor*. Indeed, *Lorna Doone* is the reason why many of Exmoor's three million annual visitors come to the park. There is a flourishing 'Dooneland' industry based around the lovely Badgworthy valley, and you can follow the Lorna Doone Trail and visit the 15th-century church at Oare where Lorna and John Ridd held their wedding, which was so tragically interrupted in the denouement of Blackmore's novel.

Blackmore, who, like his hero John Ridd, was educated at Blundell's School, Tiverton, based his romance on fact. There really was a band of outlaws named Doone who terrorised these hills, committing atrocities such as those described in his book. But as Blackmore later admitted: 'If I had dreamed that it ever

TOP, LEFT TO RIGHT: Echoes of the past in Dunster; the ford at Malmsmead, in the Doone valley

RIGHT: Statue of Lorna Doone at Dulverton

RED DEER

The red deer (Cervus elaphus) is Britain's largest and most impressive land mammal, and the Exmoor herd is descended directly from those hunted by Norman lords when the moor was a royal hunting forest. They are always a stirring sight, but especially during the autumn rut, when the majestic stags can be heard roaring (the technical and descriptive term is 'belling') across the misty coombs as they jealously gather their harem of hinds around them for mating.

The older stags live apart from the herd except for this mating period, which is usually during September and October. Calves are born in mid-June and the stags keep well away from their offspring, regrowing their magnificent antlers, which are cast off during February and March. The number of 'tines' or spikes on its antlers indicates a stag's age, and a fully mature head of antlers, with three tines on the very top, is known as a 'royal'.

TOP: *Red deer calf*

would be more than a book of the moment, the descriptions of scenery – which I know as well as I know my garden – would have been kept nearer to their fact. I romanced therein, not to mislead any other, but solely for the uses of my story.'

A PATCHWORK LANDSCAPE

Blackmore may have adapted some of the scenes of his beloved Exmoor for the purposes of his plot, but an earlier entrepreneur, John Knight, an ironmaster from Worcestershire, changed the Exmoor scene forever. He purchased 15,000 acres (6,070ha) of the moor following the passing of an Enclosure Act in 1818, intending, like the modern farmers a century and a half later, to improve it for cropping and agriculture. Knight and his son, Frederic, largely transformed Exmoor into the landscape we know today. The patchwork quilt of rectangular fields hedged with windblown beeches planted on earthen banks, the woodlands in the coombs and the moorland 'outover' above owe much to the Knights, who reclaimed about 2,500 acres (1,000ha) of moorland and built 20 miles (32km) of roads.

It is said that before the Knights came to Exmoor there was only one house in the former Royal Forest of Exmoor, which had been set aside in Norman times for the hunting of the moor's famed red deer and other game. Administered from the 11th-century keep of the de Mohun's Dunster Castle, the hunting forest was the earliest form of landscape protection on Exmoor, but its history goes back much further.

The moor is dotted with standing stones, like the Long Stone near Challacombe, and the 300-plus round barrows dating from the Bronze Age that seem to punctuate every hilltop. A string of these, marked on Ordnance Survey maps with a star-shaped symbol and Gothic lettering, can be traced along the ridgetop of The Chains, showing that it was important to these first settlers to know that their ancestors were watching over them.

Later, hill-forts, the characteristic Iron Age symbol, were built for much the same purpose and to overawe potential attackers at places like Wind Hill, Countisbury and Shoulsbury near Challacombe. They may also have been used as summer shielings, where a watch could be kept over grazing livestock.

Those earliest inhabitants undoubtedly hunted Exmoor's most impressive and ancient mammal, the stately red deer (see panel, opposite), and it is a stag's head that provides the National Park Authority with its logo. There are still more red deer on Exmoor than anywhere else in England, and they were hunted continuously since the days of the first prehistoric settlers. The creation of the Royal Forest of Exmoor nearly a thousand years ago gave them some protection, allowing only royal parties to hunt them.

Stag hunting has been a traditional Exmoor sport for many centuries, but the 2005 ban on hunting with dogs means that the Exmoor herd of around 2,700 animals has to be culled under licence by about 500 annually, to prevent damage to farmers' corn and root crops.

Alongside the red deer, the shaggy-coated Exmoor ponies (see panel, page 37) can often be seen grazing the high pastures. It is the strong farming community of Exmoor that keeps this breed alive, as it has the distinctive Red Ruby Devon beef cattle and the curly-horned, woolly Exmoor Horn sheep.

ABOVE: Dunster Castle

The main market centre for the farming community is Dunster, and it was the medieval woollen industry that gave the town its initial importance as a market. The wool trade is still visible in the form of the octagonal yarn market, built in 1609 and watched over by the massive tower of Dunster Castle. Dunster is both the eastern gateway to the national park and an excellent centre for exploring the north coast and the Brendon Hills.

Dulverton village, lying in the valley of the River Barle at the southern tip of the park, is another bustling market town of winding medieval streets. Granted its charter in 1306 by Edward I, it is now the administrative headquarters of the Exmoor National Park Authority, the modern successor to Edward's royal forest wardens. Its offices occupy the old workhouse, and there is an information centre on the premises.

The villages of Lynton and Lynmouth, scene of the flood of 1952 (see panel, opposite), are linked by a cliff railway that was opened in 1890 and has been saving visitors' legs ever since. They are the natural bases for exploration of the coast, the Valley of the Rocks and the central moorland heights. The Lyn and Exmoor Museum in Lynton gives a good insight into the area.

ABOVE: The flower-bedecked harbour at Lynmouth

LYNMOUTH FLOOD

The ferocious power of the rivers that rush off Exmoor in the short, steep journey to the Bristol Channel was tragically illustrated on the night of 15 August 1952 – an event that puts the 2004 floods at Boscastle and elsewhere into perspective.

That night, 9in (23cm) of rain fell in just five hours over The Chains. It was estimated that a staggering 3,000 million tons of rainwater fell in the 38 square miles (98sq km) drained by the East and West Lyn rivers. All that water had to go somewhere, and

inevitably it was channelled into the narrow Glen Lyn Gorge, where the Hoar Oak Water at Watersmeet joins the East Lyn. The flood uprooted trees and 10-ton boulders in its path as it rushed down towards the coastal town of Lynmouth. Roads and bridges were torn up and houses demolished by the wall of floodwater, which was estimated to be 50ft (15m) high.

Many people died in the flood, and the delta of stones and boulders can still be seen stretching out into Lynmouth Bay.

TOP: The devastating Lynmouth flood

ABOVE: The cliff railway linking Lynton and Lynmouth

NEW FOREST

If there's one thing that can be said with certainty about the New Forest – that astonishing survival of 220 square miles (570sq km) of Old England sandwiched between Southampton Water and Salisbury Plain – is that it's anything but 'new'.

A LITTLE BIT OF OLD ENGLAND

The first British national parks came into being some 60 years ago, but the New Forest was set aside as a place meriting special protection in 1079 – over nine centuries earlier. Just 13 years after the Battle of Hastings, William the Conqueror (c1027–87) designated what he called *Nova Foresta* as a royal hunting reserve, with a strict code of laws for the protection of game. It was recorded as such in two descriptive pages in the comprehensive Domesday survey, which was published seven years later.

However, in Norman times the word 'forest' did not necessarily refer to a heavily wooded area, but to land that had been confiscated by the King so that it could be used exclusively for hunting. Local people who were unfortunate enough to find themselves within William's *Nova Foresta* were not able to protect their crops and hedges, or take timber to use for their houses or fires and, most particularly, they were not allowed to hunt or trap any of the abundant game, so families often went hungry. The penalties inflicted on any luckless offenders were swingeing, and could involve mutilation or even death.

But more recent research has thrown considerable doubt on the severity of William's high-handed clearance of the Forest for his sport. Many guidebooks still tell the story of how the homes, the churches and the villages of the Forest were laid waste by the Conqueror so he could enjoy his hunting unrestricted. But the Domesday Book, for example, records the compensation paid, almost on modern lines, to owners whose land had been put under forest law. Furthermore, there is no evidence that Forest villages and churches were destroyed and laid to ruin to make room for the King's royal hunting preserve.

Indeed, the remaining older Forest churches, such as those at Brockenhurst, Breamore and Milford, may be produced as evidence that they were untouched by the Conqueror when he set up his royal forest. So perhaps some of the history books have been less than accurate.

In the Domesday survey, much of the New Forest was described as infertile woodland and furzy waste – 'furze' being the local name for the golden-flowered bushes of pineapple-scented

LEFT: Ponies seek shade from the summer sun

gorse, which still blossoms all year round on the Forest's higher and drier ground. The miracle is that, more than nine centuries later, modern visitors still enjoy large areas of landscape and scenery that would have been familiar to William of Normandy as he hunted red and fallow deer, which he is said to have loved 'as if he was their father'.

Ironically, William's son, known as Rufus for his red hair and ruddy complexion, inherited his father's passion and died in what was presumed, at the time, to have been a hunting accident in the Forest near Canterton in 1100 (see panel, page 60).

THE VERDERERS

The New Forest joined the family of British national parks in March 2005 – the ninth park in England and, most significantly, the first in the crowded southeast of Britain. It is also one of the smallest and the most densely populated of the parks, attracting more visitors from the surrounding towns and cities per square mile than any other.

Omitted from John Dower's original list of possible national parks over 60 years before – he considered that the largest landowner, the Forestry Commission, already offered adequate protection – the New Forest National Park met with considerable local objections in its planning stages.

Chief among the objectors was the ancient Court of Verderers, an august body of 10 local farmers and landowners who still administer the system of commoning, which governs grazing and other rights to the 148 square miles (383sq km) included in the 'perambulation' of the central, ancient Forest (see panel, opposite). When William the Conqueror set up his hunting preserve, despite all those other restrictions, he conceded that local people could keep their grazing rights in the Forest, and it is these rights, administered by the verderers, that the 350 existing commoners retain for their ponies, cattle and pigs.

The court, which meets every two months in the Verderers' Hall at the Queen's House in Lyndhurst, is a relic from the days of William's royal hunting forest, and probably the oldest court of law in Britain. The verderers' view on the New Forest being

ABOVE: Ober Water meanders through woodland at Puttles Bridge

THE VERDERERS

The New Forest verderers are direct descendants of William the Conqueror's foresters, who were charged with administering the ancient forest laws to protect the game and its habitat.

The Court of Verderers, which consists of 10 local farmers, landowners and commoners, meets every two months in the Verderers' Hall at the Queen's House in Lyndhurst, and administers the system of commoning which governs grazing and other rights to the Forest. The five Rights of Common, which all commoners enjoy, are:

• Pasture: the right to graze cattle, ponies, donkeys and sheep.

• Mast: the right to turn pigs out in the autumn to feed on acorns and beech mast.

• Estovers: the right to gather wood for fuel.

• Marl: the right to take limey clay as a fertiliser.

• Turbary: the right to cut turf for burning.

Five green-coated agisters are employed by the verderers to supervise the 7,000 or so grazing animals – including ponies, cattle, donkeys and pigs – which are currently kept in the Forest. Nowadays, the penalties for infringement are usually fines.

They also deal with the day-to-day management of the animals. Recognising the important on-the-ground presence of the agisters and the fact that, uniquely, it employs no rangers, the New Forest National Park Authority recently paid for new green Land Rovers for them. They have become the public face of the park.

ABOVE: The ornate west door of Lyndhurst's church

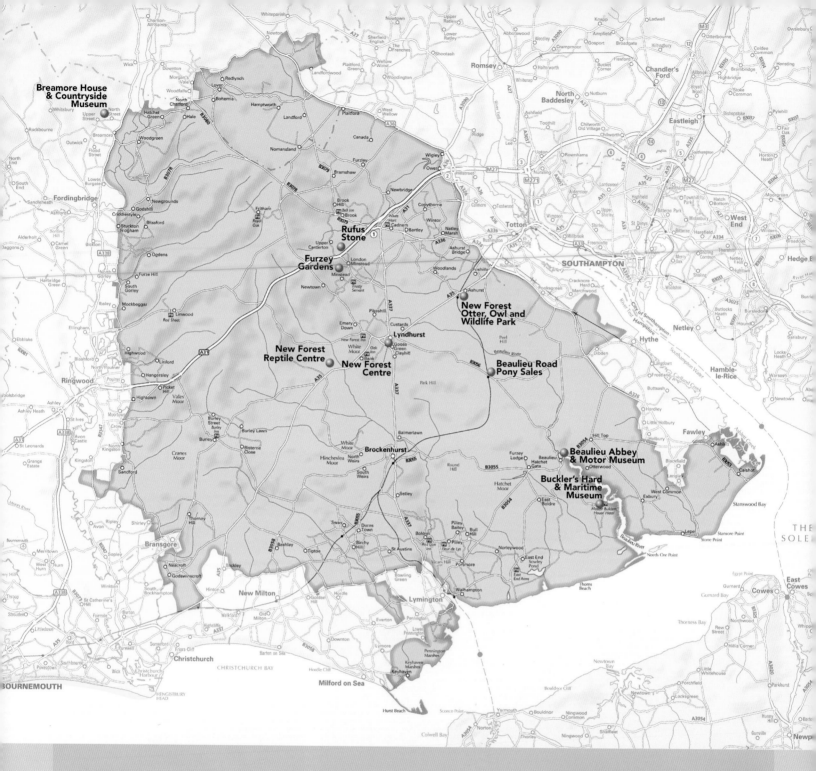

TOP SIGHTS

1. *Beaulieu Abbey and Motor Museum:* Lord Montagu's home houses a museum telling the story of motoring.

2. *Beaulieu Road Pony Sales, Lyndhurst–Beaulieu road:* site of pony sales four times a year.

3. *Breamore House and Countryside Museum:* housed in an Elizabethan manor.

4. *Buckler's Hard and Maritime Museum:* a time-warp 18th-century shipyard village.

5. *Furzey Gardens, near Minstead:* informal, pesticide-free gardens created in the 1920s.

6. *New Forest Centre, Lyndhurst:* perfect starting point for exploring the Forest.

7. *New Forest Otter, Owl and Wildlife Park, near Ashurst:* otters and owls, of course, plus foxes, lynxes, wild boar and more.

8. *New Forest Reptile Centre, near Lyndhurst:* see snakes and lizards at close quarters.

9. *Rufus Stone, Canterton:* where William II was killed in 1100.

designated a national park was: 'We have looked after the Forest perfectly well for 900 years; why change things?' Eventually, after more disputes about its western boundary, the New Forest National Park Authority assumed full powers in April 2006.

LOCAL CHARACTERS

The New Forest seems to breed independent characters and one of the most memorable was Mary Ann Girling, who in 1873 established a religious group known as the Shakers at New Forest Lodge, Vaggs Lane, near Hordle. This group of extremist Quaker nonconformists got their name from the fact that during periods of worship, usually led by Mary Ann, they could go into a trance-like state that made them seem to dance, shaking their limbs uncontrollably.

But Mary Ann was not so adept at managing the group's financial affairs, and 10 days before Christmas in 1874, the authorities evicted them from New Forest Lodge, throwing the 140 men, women and children and all their goods onto the road outside.

This attracted a good deal of local resentment, and articles appeared in the national press. Local people took in the children, and the adults were housed in a farmer's barn. Mary Ann Girling died of cancer in 1886. Apparently, she never fully recovered from the shock and exposure of her eviction, and the Shaker colony disappeared.

Another New Forest character who often hit the national headlines was Harry (or Henry) 'Brusher' Mills, the celebrated snake catcher. Mills was born in 1840 and became a forester like most other local men. Then he discovered that good money could be made out of supplying live reptiles to people like Lord Londesborough at Lyndhurst and the Zoological Gardens in London, who apparently fed them to other, snake-eating animals.

By 1889, just five years after he started his new career as a snake catcher, Brusher Mills boasted he had captured 2,000 adders and he was becoming something of a local celebrity, featuring in magazines such as the popular *Boy's Own Paper*. Many visitors

TOP: Buckler's Hard
LEFT: Palace House at Beaulieu

ABOVE, LEFT TO RIGHT: Rhododendrons on the Rhinefield Ornamental Drive; guelder rose berries; the Beaulieu River

would seek out this colourful, bearded character who lived in a crude hut, like those used by charcoal burners, in the depths of the Forest. He used a long pole to probe the undergrowth, then a pair of long-handled tongs to catch the snakes, which were very common on the Forest's heathlands. He wisely always wore knee-high boots for his own protection.

No one is exactly sure how Brusher Mills got his nickname: some say it was because he brushed the ice clean for skaters on Foxlease Lake in the winter, and then in the summer he brushed the pitch for Lyndhurst Cricket Club. Brusher Mills died in 1905, and it has been estimated that he disposed of between 30,000 and 35,000 adders during his lifetime. He is buried in Brockenhurst churchyard under a carved headstone, which shows him at work.

WILDLIFE UNDER THREAT

Within the park's boundaries is one of the rare surviving areas of lowland heath in Britain. The rapid development of the countryside, especially in the southeast, has seen most of this nationally important habitat swallowed up at an alarming rate, and today only about 24,270 acres (9,822ha) remain – around a sixth of the area that existed here in 1800.

The pressure for development is still on. There are plans to build 80,000 new houses on the eastern boundary of the park and 30,000 on the western boundary within the next 20 years. With Britain's largest oil refinery on Southampton Water to the east and the threat of extension to Bournemouth airport in the south, it is no surprise to find that the 60 staff of the New Forest National Park Authority deal with the highest number of planning applications of any British national park.

ABOVE, LEFT TO RIGHT: Snoozing sika deer... and rather more alert fallow deer on the plains near Stoney Cross

ABOVE: *Sunrise over Southampton Water, seen from Calshot in the southeast corner of the Forest*

AUTUMN LEAVES

There's no doubt that one of the best times to visit the New Forest is in the autumn, when the changing colours of the leaves make it a sight to rival the fabled 'Fall' of New England.

As the sap is gradually cut off from the bosky green leaves of high summer, beeches change to a burnished gold, chestnuts turn bright yellow, maples blush scarlet, and oaks and ashes curl up and go brown.

There's a bonus for wildlife in the berries produced at this time of the year too. The hedges are laden with the bright scarlet berries of hips and haws of the wild rose and hawthorn, while the multicoloured beads of bryony drape artistically around the wispy strands of old man's beard, or traveller's joy. Elsewhere, luscious chandeliers of ebony elderberries hang like grapes in a vineyard, and the tiny plums of the blackthorn (or sloes) take on an attractive blue bloom.

You can witness a wonderful display of kaleidoscopic autumn colours almost anywhere within the New Forest, but among the best sites are in the Ancient and Ornamental Woodlands, such as Godshill, Bolderwood and Rhinefield.

Yet, despite these pressures, this precious wilderness survives. The New Forest is home to Britain's largest native land mammal, the red deer, and large herds of fallow and sika deer graze the open, grassy clearings, known as 'lawns', among the trees. It is a scene virtually unchanged for nine centuries, and that's a real rarity in Britain today.

To stand a good chance of catching a glimpse of the deer, go to places such as the sanctuary at Bolderwood and wait quietly until twilight when they generally leave the security of their daytime cover. If you keep to your car you are more likely to get a view because most deer, and fallows in particular, seem unconcerned about a parked vehicle.

And if you come across an unaccountably muddy patch surrounded by trees that have been slashed and mutilated in the middle of the Forest, you will have encountered the rutting scrape of a stag or buck. During the autumn rutting season, males will wallow in this mucky bath so that they become completely plastered with mud, then they thrash the surrounding trees and vegetation to add further 'adornment' to their antlers with which to tempt a mate.

All six of Britain's native reptiles, of which the smooth snake and sand lizard are now reckoned to be exceptionally rare, can be found on the Forest's heathlands. The temperate weather is perfectly suited to the lifestyle of reptiles, and there is a reptilary, the New Forest Reptile Centre, founded by leading keeper Derek Thomson, at Holidays Hill, off the A35 near Rhinefield. Visit on a warm day to be sure of seeing the reptiles basking in the sun in their open-air pens.

The snake you are most likely to come across in the Forest is the adder or viper, with its distinctive zigzag markings. Although Britain's only poisonous species, the adder is a shy and retiring creature and will only strike if provoked. If you are really lucky,

TOP: Bolderwood, where there is a deer sanctuary and one of the oldest trees in Britain – the Knightwood Oak

ABOVE, LEFT TO RIGHT: Adder with its young; one of the 2,700 species of fungi in the park; turnstone, a familiar shore bird

ABOVE: *Rockford Common*

AN ANCIENT WHODUNNIT

The three-sided, cast-iron monument known as the Rufus Stone at Canterton, just off the A31 near Stoney Cross, marks the spot of one of the most famous 'whodunnits' in British history. It was here, in 1100, that an oak tree deflected the arrow which fatally injured King William II, known as Rufus.

The man who took the fateful shot at a fleeing stag was Sir William Tyrell, and there is a pub nearby at Upper Canterton that still bears his name.

Historians have debated for years whether it was an accident or a deliberate act of murder by Tyrell. He certainly aroused suspicion by immediately fleeing the scene to return to his native Normandy, while Rufus's brother Henry, also in the hunting party, set off hotfoot to Winchester to claim the throne.

No one seems to have mourned Rufus's death, because it seems he was generally disliked and apparently responsible for the clearing of many villages within the Forest so that he could enjoy his hunting unobstructed.

One theory postulates that Rufus had blocked Henry's proposed marriage to Eadgyth, daughter of the King of Scotland, making him a wanted man, while another claims he was a 'witch king' of the heretic Catharist faith and actually willed his own death to atone for the sins of the world.

you might just witness the fabled 'adders' dance'. This occurs in the breeding season (April and May) when two competing males rear up and engage in a vertical spiralling dance.

The Forest plays host to a rich population of heath-loving birds, such as Britain's only resident warbler, the perky, red-eyed Dartford warbler, which can be seen perched on the highest branches of a gorse bush tut-tutting its warning call. One bird you may hear as evening falls is the secretive nightjar, a hawk-like summer visitor known locally as a night hawk. It is one of the great wildlife experiences of the New Forest to stand out on the heath as dusk falls and listen to the deep, resonant, churring call of this moth-hunting bird.

In wetter areas, the valleys (or 'bottoms') of the Forest are alive with the song of waders such as redshank, curlew and lapwing. In the evening, the strange 'drumming' sound of the secretive snipe echoes around the rides. Birds of prey include the dashing, sickle-winged hobby, the soaring buzzard, fierce sparrowhawks and hovering kestrels. In winter, the graceful, ghostly shapes of hen harriers quarter the heathlands in search of small mammals.

But the Forest, like all the other British national parks, is essentially a living and working landscape. It is also one of the most heavily populated of the parks, with a resident population of about 34,400. Most inhabitants live in the bustling villages of Brockenhurst, Burley and Beaulieu.

The only town within the park is Lyndhurst – the ancient capital of the New Forest, its administrative centre (the Court of Verderers, see panel, page 51, meets here) and a busy tourist hub. Here the New Forest Centre museum provides a perfect introduction to the park with displays and exhibitions.

The Forestry Commission has managed the forested area – about half of the park – since 1924 as Crown Land, and it still employs about 100 people, producing around 40,000 tonnes of timber annually. The New Forest Act of 1877 recognised that some parts of the Forest were of great amenity value, and designated them to be 'Ancient and Ornamental Woodlands', where the medieval character of the Forest was retained, managed by foresters and still grazed by the commoners' animals. Examples of these woodlands can be found around Godshill, Bolderwood, Knightwood, Rhinefield, Wilverley and Canterton.

There are few places left in Europe, let alone Britain, where this ancient regime of woodland pasture management still exists. Oliver Rackham, an expert on the history of British woodland, describes woodland pasture as the use of the same land both for trees and for grazing animals. This apparent contradiction – the more trees there are the less grazing, and animals will usually eat saplings – has been practised for more than 1,200 years, but the New Forest is one of the last surviving examples in Britain where cattle and pigs can still be seen foraging for food among the trees.

TOP: The Rufus Stone

NEW FOREST PONIES

One of the commonest sights you are likely to encounter as you drive through the Forest is ponies grazing peacefully by the side of the road. However, despite the warning signs and speed limits many animals are killed every year and visitors are asked not to feed the ponies as it encourages them to the roadside.

There are thought to be about 4,000 ponies living in the Forest today, all of which are privately owned. They are rounded up in 'drifts' in late summer or early autumn when distinctive cuts are made in their long, flowing tails to show which district of the Forest they belong to.

Although descended from primitive native ponies similar to the Exmoor and Dartmoor breeds, the New Forest pony has been subject to controlled breeding and improvement over the years. In 1850, for example, Queen Victoria lent stallions to the verderers in order to improve the breeding pool, and since World War II the stock has been improved considerably.

New Forest ponies are usually docile creatures with a reliable temperament, and as a result make excellent riding ponies for children – although they are also capable of carrying adults. They stand from 12.2 to 14.2 hands (4ft/1.2m to 4.5ft/1.4m) high, and may be any colour except piebald, skewbald, spotted or blue-eyed cream.

Sales of the ponies are held annually in April, August, September and October at the Lyndhurst–Beaulieu road junction near Beaulieu Road railway station. This is an important social gathering for Forest dwellers, as well as being the main chance for owners to buy and sell their stock.

ABOVE: A pony sale at Beaulieu

SOUTH DOWNS

Peals of bells rang out from flint-faced village churches along the length of the rolling South Downs on Friday 1 April 2011. This was no April Fool's Day joke, nor did it mark the imminent royal wedding. The joyful chorus heralded the creation of Britain's latest, longest and busiest national park.

INTRINSIC MERITS

The case for the designation of the South Downs as a national park can be traced back well over 60 years to the 1947 Hobhouse report. The report stated that it was convinced of the importance of including at least one national park within easy reach of London.

> There exists in the South Downs an area of still unspoilt country, certainly of less wildness and grandeur than the more rugged Parks of the north and west, but possessing great natural beauty and much open rambling land, extending south-eastward to the magnificent chalk cliffs of Beachy Head and Seven Sisters. We recommend it unhesitatingly on its intrinsic merits as well as on the grounds of its accessibility.

Most people seemed to agree, but it was not until April 2000 that the former Countryside Agency – now Natural England – began the process of designating the South Downs as a national park. After a 16-month-long public inquiry, mainly concerned with its boundaries, country lovers throughout Britain were delighted to hear in March 2010 that the South Downs had finally been designated as England's 10th and Britain's 15th national park.

Covering an area of 636 square miles (1,648sq km), this largely linear park extends for over 100 miles (160km) from the edge of the ancient cathedral city of Winchester in east Hampshire in the west, to the dramatic 530ft (162m) dazzlingly white cliffs of Beachy Head and the Seven Sisters, on the outskirts of Eastbourne in Sussex, in the east. It is about 10 miles (16km) wide at its broadest, between Haslemere in the north and Chichester in the south.

The linear nature of the park and its proximity to London and the large cities and resorts of the South Coast – such as Portsmouth, Bognor Regis, Littlehampton, Worthing, Brighton and Newhaven – mean that it has a large amount of through traffic every day. This has resulted in an estimated day visitor count of 39 million, making it by far the most visited of all Britain's national parks. In 2007, the estimated population was nearly 108,000 – making it also the most heavily populated of the family of British parks.

LEFT: The cliffs of Beachy Head with the red-and-white striped lighthouse

The South Downs National Park was created by an amalgamation of the former Sussex Downs and East Hampshire Areas of Outstanding Natural Beauty (AONBs), which had been designated in 1965 and 1961 respectively.

THE ROCKS BENEATH

All the rocks that form the South Downs are sedimentary; that is, laid down as sediment created by the remains of tiny crustaceans, sand or mud either under the sea or in freshwater lakes, which was gradually compressed and hardened into rock. Most of these rocks were formed around 120 million years ago during the Cretaceous period, relatively recently in British geological terms. The geology of the park is a combination of the dark greensands and clays of the Weald around Haslemere, and the shining white chalk spine of the Downs.

Archaeologist Jacquetta Hawkes, in her perceptive book *A Land* (1951), painted a vivid picture of the way chalk was formed in

ABOVE: The view over the rolling Downs at Devil's Dyke, near Brighton

that ancient Cretaceous sea: 'I like to think of the seas where chalk was forming clouded with white as though from a snow storm – a fall that lasted for thirty million years and lay to a depth of a thousand feet.'

Lying within the beds of chalk are bands of nodules of harder crystalline quartz known as flint, which shines blue-black when chipped or 'knapped' and is used as the facing of buildings, such as the splendid West Dean College near Chichester or the various medieval church towers and barns within the park. Found in many downland villages, it is sometimes known as 'Sussex diamonds'. It is thought that flint formed from the skeletal remains of sponges within the chalk, which used silica rather than calcium carbonate to construct their skeletons.

This sandwich of sedimentary rocks was uplifted by archaic earth movements around 75 million years ago into a huge dome, some 125 miles (201km) long and 50 miles (80km) wide. This dome was then inexorably worn away, mainly by swollen meltwater rivers such as the modern Arun, the Rother and the Meon, at the end of the Ice Age to form the contrasting uplands of the South Downs and the lowland plain of the Weald. The Devil's Dyke, a scrub-covered cleft slicing through the Downs near Fulking, is also thought to have been formed by these erosive glacial meltwaters. But the dominating landscape feature of the national park is the steep, northward-facing scarp of the South Downs; what local resident Rudyard Kipling (1865–1936) described as 'Our blunt, bow-headed, whale-backed Downs' in his 1900 poem, *Sussex*. From this high crest – which reaches 889ft (271m) at Butser Hill near Petersfield, 830ft (253m) at Crown Tegleaze near East Lavington, and 814ft (248m) at Ditchling Beacon near Westmeston – gentle slopes of former downland, now mostly extensively farmed for cereals, dip gradually away to the coastal plain and the Channel coast.

The East Hampshire part of the park is a country of two halves. The River Meon, with its ancient British name, forms the boundary, with the rolling chalk Downs around High Cross and Empshott in the north and west, and the deeply wooded scarps and heaths more usually associated with Surrey and Sussex taking up the eastern half. The rich and fertile Meon and Rother river valleys, with their deep, flower-filled lanes and colour-washed, half-timbered villages, form the centrepiece.

The high crest of the Downs is scalloped by richly wooded coombs or dry valleys – known here as 'bottoms' – while at their eastern extremity, they reach the sea in a glorious flourish at the magnificent white cliffs and cut-off hanging valleys of the Seven Sisters, near Cuckmere, and the soaring 530ft (162m) cliff of Beachy Head, the highest chalk cliff in Britain, south of Eastbourne.

Construction of the lighthouse known as Belle Tout, on top of the next headland west of Beachy Head, began in 1831 and it became operational three years later. But the frequent Channel mists and low clouds could obscure the light, so it was decided that another lighthouse needed to be built on the shore below Beachy Head, and this was completed in 1902. Belle Tout was converted to a private residence, but the constantly crumbling chalk cliffs resulted in it being bodily moved more than 56ft (17m) further inland in March 1999. It is now an exclusive hotel.

The 140ft (43m) high red-and-white striped lighthouse built in 1902 at the foot of Beachy Head is one of the most famous landmarks in the national park. For over 80 years, the tower was manned by a team of three lighthouse keepers whose job was to maintain the light, which rotates with two white flashes every 20 seconds and is visible 26 miles (42km) out to sea. The lighthouse was automated in 1983 and the keepers were withdrawn.

ABOVE, LEFT TO RIGHT: Looking over surrounding countryside from the Fulking escarpment; cycling along a track at Ditchling

TOP SIGHTS

1 Arundel Castle, Arundel: family seat of the Dukes of Norfolk for over 400 years.

2 Beachy Head: highest chalk cliff in Britain (530ft/162m), with a lighthouse at its foot.

3 Butser Hill Ancient Farm, near Petersfield: open-air archaeological museum and working replica of an Iron Age farm.

4 Chanctonbury Ring, near Findon: mysterious Iron Age hill-fort topped by a ring of beeches that were decimated by the 1987 hurricane.

5 Kingley Vale NNR, West Stoke: the largest yew forest in Europe, with stunning views to be had from its downland summit.

6 Lewes Castle and town: busy market town and 'capital' of the South Downs.

7 Long Man of Wilmington, near Wilmington: largest human representation in a chalk figure in Britain, thought to date from Saxon times.

8 Petworth House (NT), Petworth: vast 17th-century mansion set in a 700-acre (283ha) deer park

landscaped by Capability Brown.

9 Seven Sisters, near Cuckmere: iconic series of hanging valleys cut into chalk cliffs.

10 Uppark House (NT), near Petersfield: imposing 17th-century mansion situated on an elevated site near Petersfield, lovingly restored after a disastrous fire in 1989.

11 The Wakes, Selborne: home of the Reverend Gilbert White, pioneering 18th-century observer of nature.

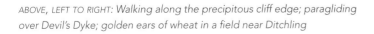

ABOVE, LEFT TO RIGHT: Walking along the precipitous cliff edge; paragliding over Devil's Dyke; golden ears of wheat in a field near Ditchling

DOWNLAND WILDLIFE

The few remaining patches of unimproved herb-rich chalk grassland on the Downs, such as the nature reserves at Ditchling Beacon, Kingley Vale and Old Winchester Hill, are nationally important wildlife habitats.

The 50-acre (20ha) Sussex Wildlife Trust nature reserve at Ditchling Beacon, on the site of an Iron Age hillfort, features fragrant, common spotted and twayblade orchids, marjoram, thyme and many other chalk grassland flowers, which in turn support colonies of brown argus, green hairstreak, common blue and chalkhill blue butterflies.

The National Nature Reserve (NNR) of Kingley Vale, on the southern edge of the Downs near West Stoke, contains one of the finest and largest native yew woodlands in Europe, and was one of the first NNRs to be established in Britain in 1952. But the reserve itself is a mere stripling compared with the age of some of the venerable yews for which it is famous. Many have probably already celebrated their 500th birthday, and some may be as old as 1,000 years. A walk through these incredibly ancient trees transports you through an Arthur Rackham-like landscape of tortured, twisted trunks and dark, cave-like clearings, where you half expect to see fairies appear at every turn.

From the top of the coomb above the trees, the southern views extend to the elegant spire of Chichester Cathedral and the snaking inlets of Chichester Harbour, with the silvery glint of the English Channel and the misty blue outline of the Isle of Wight beyond.

Two Bronze Age burial mounds known as the Devil's Humps, the reputed last resting place of a pair of kings (hence the name of the valley), mark the summit. There is also a simple sarsen standing stone in memory of the pioneering ecologist Sir Arthur Tansley (1871–1955), the first chairman of the Nature Conservancy Council. Tansley loved this place, claiming it was his favourite viewpoint in the whole of Britain, and few would argue with his choice.

Old Winchester Hill, near Meonstoke, is another NNR which provides a rich mosaic of chalkland habitats. These range from hawthorn scrub and small yew and juniper woods to the open chalk downland which is so important for native butterflies such as the chalkhill blue, dark green fritillary and the rare Duke of Burgundy.

In contrast, the rich flood meadows of Amberley Wild Brooks, near Amberley, which are part of the Arun Valley Special Protection Area (SPA), are vital over-wintering wetlands for a number of species of wildfowl, including Bewick swans, wigeon and teal. They also support extremely important breeding populations of lapwings, redshanks, and the only sizeable Sussex population of snipe.

TOP, LEFT TO RIGHT: Wigeon; brown hare; redshank
RIGHT: The view westwards across heather from Black Down

ABOVE, LEFT TO RIGHT: Polo players at Cowdray Park; the famous Bonfire Night procession at Lewes

THE LITERARY DOWNS

The South Downs have attracted writers and artists over many years. Rottingdean was the home of Edward Burne-Jones and his nephew Rudyard Kipling, whose poem Sussex is quoted earlier in this chapter, and who wrote the Just So Stories and Stalky and Co while living there.

Virginia and Leonard Woolf lived at Monk's House, Rodmell, and Virginia's last novel, Between the Acts, is thought to have been inspired by the ancient farm buildings and old Clergy House at Alfriston, now in the care of the National Trust.

But perhaps the most remarkable of the artistic colonies in the South Downs was at Ditchling. The pivotal figure was the artist–craftsman Eric Gill, type-designer, wood engraver and social reformer, who lived in the village between 1907–13, before moving to Hopkin's Crank on Ditchling Common, where he built a chapel and workshops.

H. G. Wells' mother was a lady's maid at Uppark House, where he immersed himself in its wonderful library, reading the classics which introduced him to the world of literature. Wells was later sent as a boarder to Midhurst Grammar School for a short period, later becoming a student teacher there.

Other writers who have been inspired by the Downs include Hilaire Belloc, who was brought up in the delightful village of Slindon, which he regarded as the jewel in the downland crown, and Vanessa Bell, who, when living at Charleston farmhouse, attracted many members of the infamous Bloomsbury Group, including Clive Bell, Lytton Strachey, E. M. Forster and Maynard Keynes.

Henry III and Simon de Montfort, in which de Montfort's forces were victorious.

At the time of the Marian Persecutions of 1555–57, Lewes was the scene of the execution of 17 Protestant martyrs, who were burnt at the stake in front of the Star Inn, which is now the Town Hall. Lewes developed as the county town of East Sussex throughout the 17th and 18th centuries, expanding beyond the limits of the original town wall.

But Lewes is probably best known today for the largest and most famous Bonfire Night celebration in the country. A highlight of the Lewes Bonfire, held annually on Guy Fawkes' Day (5 November), is the somewhat controversial burning of an effigy of the Pope. The reason for this is that in Lewes the event also commemorates the memory of those Protestants who were burnt at the stake at the time of the 16th-century Marian Persecutions.

There are many small villages in the national park, such as Clayton, with its two windmills known as Jack and Jill, Steyning (pronounced Stenning), West and East Meon, Meonstoke and Warnford, all of which have a wealth of traditional buildings in brick, flint, chalk and half-timbering, reflecting the predominant building materials of the South Downs.

A few miles north of Petersfield on the B3006 is the small village of Selborne, famous as the home and outdoor laboratory of the Reverend Gilbert White, the 18th-century pioneer in the study of natural history (see panel, page 70). An excellent museum explains his work, and that of the Antarctic explorer Captain Titus Oates, who also lived in Selborne. Selborne Hill and The Hanger, reached by a hedged, zigzag path constructed by White, is now a National Trust property, and the visitor can still enjoy the view of the village that he did, through the magnificent 'hanging' beech, wych elm and lime trees.

White would almost certainly have approved of the South Downs National Park as it was designated because of the importance of places such as Selborne and the herb-rich flora of the unimproved downland pastures further to the north and west.

Today, the chief industry in the national park is agriculture, with large, mainly arable holdings on the chalk Downs and mixed or dairy farming in the river valleys. The clear chalk rivers of the Meon and Rother have been famous for their trout fishing ever since Izaak Walton, author of *The Compleat Angler*, stayed at East Meon to fish there in the 17th century. The 99-mile (160km) South Downs Way National Trail runs the length of the park from Eastbourne to Winchester, and there is a wealth of other public footpaths which allow the visitor to thoroughly explore the area.

TOP: *H. G. Wells grew up at Uppark House, where his mother was a maid*
RIGHT: *The crystal-clear waters of the River Itchen*

ABOVE: Distant Blackcap hill seen across poppy fields

THE BROADS

Moving silently between the swaying reedbeds of Barton Broad under the billowing sail of *Hathor*, one of a handful of wherries still plying the Broads, it's hard to imagine that the tranquil landscape through which you are passing is anything but natural.

MADE BY MAN

The peaceful lakes and waterways, fringed by tawny reedbeds, are alive with birds and insects and appear untouched by man. Only the graceful landmarks of white-sailed windpumps and the occasional flint-faced tower of a medieval church peeping over clumps of woodland seem to signify human influence.

That is the great paradox of the Norfolk and Suffolk Broads. Like so many British landscapes, even this apparently untouched 'natural' landscape was once the scene of great human industry. And unlike any other British national park, it was man-made. This astonishing discovery – perhaps the British equivalent to John Muir's controversial disclosure that Yosemite Valley in the USA was actually excavated by glaciers and not the result of a gigantic geological fault – was made around 50 years ago by a team comprising a botanist, a geomorphologist, a geographer, an archaeologist and a civil engineer.

The group of academics – Joyce Lambert, J. N. Jennings, C. T. Smith, Charles Green and J. N. Hutchinson – published their findings to the Royal Geographical Society in a paper

entitled *The Making of the Broads* in 1960. The paper showed conclusively that the Broads were not, as had been previously thought, lakes formed after the sea had flooded into natural peaty hollows, but that those hollows had been the direct result of large-scale medieval peat extraction.

The extent of that extraction was deduced by meticulous examination of the records of St Benet's Abbey, a Benedictine monastery on the banks of the River Bure at Holme, near Ludham. The scanty flint-faced ruin of St Benet's, now dominated by the remains of an 18th-century, red-brick tower mill just inside the gatehouse, is one of the most important historic monuments in the Broads, and more than likely dates back to the 9th century. The abbey was rebuilt and endowed with three manors by King Canute in 1020.

The abbey's records showed that from the 12th century onwards large areas of Hoveton parish were set aside for peat digging, and in one year alone more than a million turves (blocks of peat used for fires) were cut. This industrial-scale extraction went on continuously for more than 200 years, and by the early

LEFT: Stracey Arms Mill on the River Bure, near Acle

14th century, at the height of its importance, the cathedral priory at Norwich was using nearly 400,000 turves annually from the area we now know as the Broads.

The total area excavated by those 12ft deep (3.6m) medieval peat diggings has been estimated at around 2,600 acres (1,052ha), and conclusive evidence of their human creation was provided by a study of their unnaturally steep-sided banks, cut straight through the natural peat base of the valley floors. Also, telltale narrow peninsulas and islands of peat divided some of the Broads, another clue to their creation eight centuries ago. The peat diggings were eventually joined to the main river systems when wildfowlers, fishermen and reed cutters (see panel, opposite) dug channels to link them.

But where did all the water come from? From the 13th century onwards there was a slight change in the relative levels of the land and the sea, and coastal and low-lying areas like the Broads became increasingly at risk from flooding – not unlike the effects of global warming and the predicted rise in sea levels today.

TOP: Reedbeds at Hickling

REED CUTTING

The age-old trade of reed and sedge cutting has done much to shape the landscape of the Broads. The tall Norfolk reeds, which can grow up to 10ft (3m) in height, provide valuable habitats for wildlife and have been in demand for use in thatching for centuries.

The traditional skills of reed and sedge cutting were dying out at the turn of the millennium and confidence in the industry was low. In 2003, the Broads Reed and Sedge Cutters Association (Brasca) was formed, enabling the remaining self-employed cutters to apply for grant aid to replace outdated machinery and equipment. The Broads Authority and Brasca are also training new recruits to cut reeds and sedge.

Cutting is done mostly with machinery but scythes are sometimes used. Boats were often used to transport the cut reed and sedge to the nearest staithe for transportation, but today most is moved using quad bikes and trailers.

ABOVE: Reed cutting is carried out from December to the end of March, while sedge is cut during the summer months

There were some cursory attempts to dredge peat from under the steadily rising waters, but by the 15th century peat digging was no longer practical and it was abandoned.

Tithe maps from the 1840s show that the Broads once covered nearly 3,000 acres (1,214ha) of open water. Since then, the shallow lakes formed from the peat diggings have gradually filled up with dead and dying vegetation and sediment. The total area of open water today is less than half that during the 18th century, but there are still 125 miles (200km) of lock-free, navigable rivers and broads in the national park, which are enjoyed by thousands of boaters every year.

GENESIS OF THE NATIONAL PARK

The Broads, which cover 117 square miles (305sq km) of Norfolk and Suffolk, became the 11th national park in 1989 – over 30 years after the designation of the 10th, the Brecon Beacons. The reason for the long delay was partly because John Dower's original blueprint for British national parks specifically referred to 'beautiful and relatively wild' country, and it was thought then that it could only be found in upland areas. Ideas of wilderness change, however, and supporters were delighted when the Broads became the first park in the southeastern half of England.

What they lack in crags, mountains and moorlands, the Broads make up for in their ever-changing sky and waterscapes so elegantly depicted by the famous Norwich School of artists, which included John Crome, John Sell Cotman, Henry Bright and Joseph Stannard. They were inspired by the clarity of light and the wonderful vista of clouds and water; a landscape that also inspired author Arthur Ransome (1884–1967), who set his 1934 children's book *Coot Club* here.

The catalyst for the creation of the Broads National Park was actually the threat posed by agricultural improvement, particularly on the Halvergate Marshes, that large area of low-lying grazing meadows drained by the River Yare and situated directly inland from Great Yarmouth. The traditional regime for these flood meadows had always involved the grazing of cattle, a practice which kept the marshes in good condition and encouraged other wildlife.

This good practice ended with the headlong drive for arable production during the 1980s: schemes and grants were made available to farmers to drain the marshes, lower the water table and convert them to more profitable cereal production. The process had already started before conservationists blew the whistle and the Ministry of Agriculture instituted the Broads Grazing Marsh Conservation Scheme. Later, the Broads became the first Environmentally Sensitive Area (ESA) in the country, and the marshes, broads and levels were saved for posterity.

TOP, LEFT TO RIGHT: *Kayaker on Barton Broad; the vane and sails of Thurne Mill*

ABOVE: *Oulton Broad*

TOP SIGHTS

1 *Berney Marshes and Breydon Water: RSPB reserve just inland from Great Yarmouth.*

2 *Broads Wildlife Centre, Ranworth Broad: floating visitor centre.*

3 *Burgh Castle, near Great Yarmouth: remnants of a Roman fort, overlooking Breydon Water to Berney Arms Windmill (closed).*

4 *Hickling Broad National Nature Reserve, near Potter Heigham: a patchwork of wetland habitats managed by the Norfolk Wildlife Trust.*

5 *How Hill and Toad Hole Cottage, near Ludham: see page 91.*

6 *Museum of the Broads, Stalham: tools from thatching, eel catching and boat-building; video and slide shows.*

7 *Oulton Broad: a magnet for all types of sailing and other water craft.*

8 *St Benet's Abbey, near Ludham: abbey ruins and windpump.*

WETLAND WONDERLAND

Today, the Broads are one of the most important wetland landscapes in Europe, and provide a home to many spectacular kinds of wildlife. The habitats found here can be divided into four main types: the open broads and rivers, the fens, the grazing marshes and wet, or 'carr', woodland.

Three major rivers of the Broads (the Bure, the Yare and the Waveney) drain two-thirds of Norfolk and a large part of northern Suffolk. Traditionally, the waters of the Broads supported a wide variety of plants, providing abundant shelter and food for fish, amphibians, birds and animals. Problems arose when agricultural and sewage run-off from the surrounding arable farmland and villages enriched the waters so much that it created an explosion of microscopic algae, choking out all other plant and animal life.

The Broads Authority, together with Anglian Water Services and the Environment Agency, responded to this insidious process by pumping out the enriched sediment from the bottom of the rivers. This action, when added to stricter control of agricultural chemicals, has resulted in a dramatic improvement in water quality and re-establishment of submerged water plants like water lily, hornwort and bladderwort. Moreover, the birds have returned too, so these days you might expect to see the great crested grebe, heron, shoveler, tufted and mallard ducks, or even the electric flash of the kingfisher.

The fens – wet, boggy areas on the edges of the Broads dominated by tall stands of reeds and sedge – are probably the most important areas for wildlife in the national park. In fact, they are of international importance for the wide range of plants, insects and birds they support. The rare Norfolk hawker dragonfly provides the Broads Authority with its logo, and another spectacular insect which frequents the fens is Britain's largest butterfly, the swallowtail (see panel, above).

Overhead, you may be lucky enough to see the wraith-like, ghostly shape of the marsh harrier buoyantly quartering the reedbeds in search of prey. The male can be recognised by its silver-grey tail and dark brown plumage. This is one of Britain's rarest birds of prey and the Broads are one of its remaining strongholds. Another extremely rare bird found deep in the reedbeds is the seldom seen and highly secretive bittern. Its low, booming, foghorn-like call is one of the great, truly spine-tingling sounds of the Broads. Higher up in the feathery reed heads, the dashing little bearded tit, with its striking black moustache, performs gymnastics on the stems.

The grazing marshes, such as those at Halvergate, form the heartland of the Broads. This flat area between the rivers Bure and Yare once formed part of the estuary emptying into the sea, but now lies largely below sea level and the rivers have high embankments to avoid the risk of flooding. As a result, boats often seem to glide along above the surface of the land.

Threaded by drainage ditches (locally known as dykes), which were first cut in the 14th century, the former marshes are used for grazing cattle – typically Friesians – during the summer months. In winter the land is allowed to flood, providing important feeding grounds for migrating wildfowl and waders.

LEFT: Ranworth Broad

TOP BIRDING SITES

1. *Hickling Broad: large open broad near Potter Heigham.*
2. *Ranworth Broad: showpiece broad near South Walsham.*
3. *Strumpshaw Fen (RSPB): off the A47 near Brundall.*
4. *Surlingham Church Marsh (RSPB): off the A146 near Surlingham.*
5. *Berney Marshes (RSPB): near Berney Arms Station.*

The dykes are also important for plants, such as water violet, frogbit, arrowhead and the carnivorous bladderwort. Iridescent damselflies and dragonflies flit delicately over the channels in summer, and lapwings, redshanks, snipe and wagtails nest between the grassy tussocks in the wetter, boggier meadows.

Another resident, which can often be seen standing motionless by the water's edge, is the stately heron, known locally as a harnser. These large, slate-grey-and-white birds are almost the size of a golden eagle, and their heavy, laboured flight is a common sight over the marshes. They nest communally in early spring, constructing large, untidy, stick-built platforms in the leafless trees, to which they return year after year. Some heronries are thought to be centuries old.

Herons feed on fish, eels and occasionally water voles by standing stock still for minutes on end until they see a movement on or under the water. Then they strike with lightning speed with their dagger-like bill, impaling their unfortunate prey before flapping off in a leisurely fashion to their nest or to safety. There are thought to be around 100 breeding pairs of herons in and around the Broads.

Mills, often mistakenly called windmills, punctuate the Broads' skyline, but in almost every case these are windpumps, built to drain water from the marshes. Wonderful examples can be seen at Berney Arms, Herringfleet, Turf Fen (How Hill), Boardman's Mill and Thurne Dyke. It makes you wonder if they attracted the same kind of outcry when they were erected in the 18th and 19th centuries as 21st-century modern wind turbines do today.

The low-lying land with the wind sweeping in from the North Sea makes the Broads an ideal place to use wind power. Sutton Mill, near Stalham, is the tallest tower mill in the country, with nine floors and a fascinating collection of old farm machinery and tools. The windpumps at Stracey Arms, Berney Arms and Horsey (which is now in the care of the National Trust) allow the visitor to climb the towers and appreciate the views. Some mills, like

ABOVE: *The solar-powered Broads Authority boat Ra on Barton Broad*

TOP, LEFT TO RIGHT: *Grey heron; a barn owl on the hunt*
RIGHT: *Horsey Mere*

the one at Thurne Dyke, have been extended with a cylindrical section to accommodate longer sails. This process was known as haining and, combined with the introduction of self-regulating shutters on the sails, greatly improved efficiency.

Another important wildlife habitat on the Broads is the wet or 'carr' woodland, which has been described as the closest thing Britain has to a tropical rainforest. It is characterised by wetland-loving trees such as alder, sallow and, in drier areas, silver birch. Inside, these woodlands are dense and swampy, and it is practically impossible to walk through them in any degree of comfort. Birdlife here includes woodpeckers, redpolls, siskins and blackcaps, and woodcock can be seen and heard 'roding' through the open rides. A good place to see the succession of a fen towards carr woodland is on Ranworth Broad.

An unexpected and exotic resident of the Broad's carr woodlands is the Chinese water deer. No one is absolutely sure how these shy and secretive animals came to be here, but the likelihood is that they escaped from a private collection – possibly the Duke of Bedford's Woburn Estate in the 1950s. These tiny fawn-coloured animals, only slightly bigger than a dog, do not carry antlers but the bucks have small, walrus-like tusks on their upper jaw that can be withdrawn when they are grazing on grass shoots and small plants, and brought forward for fighting other bucks, usually during the autumn rut. They have not travelled very far from the Broads, which provides them with the type of sheltering reedbeds and grasslands they prefer, but there is a high mortality rate among fawns; many die from

hypothermia or are taken by foxes. Despite that, they seem to be doing better in Norfolk than in their native China, where the species is in a steady decline.

Another foreign species that adapted quickly to life on the Broads was the South American coypu. This relative of the guinea pig is one of the largest rodents in the world, growing up to 23in (60cm) in length and weighing up to 20lbs (9kg), and has conspicuous bright orange incisor teeth. It was introduced to East Anglia in the 1920s and early 1930s and bred for its dense, soft underfur, known as nutria. Inevitably, however, some animals escaped, and when the coypu farms were closed down during World War II many more turned feral.

At one time it was thought that the coypu would prove a beneficial addition to the local fauna by eating reeds and vegetation and keeping the waterways clear. But their voracious appetite soon extended to local garden and commercial vegetables, cereal crops, potatoes and, most importantly in East Anglia, sugar beet. They also undermined the banks of waterways with their burrows, and soon became an official Ministry of Agriculture pest and were subjected to intensive trapping and shooting campaigns during the 1950s, 60s and 70s.

The coypu, however, proved to be remarkably resilient. It was not officially declared extinct until 1987, after a final campaign costing £2.5 million that involved 24 trappers setting 48 traps a day. It is a good example of the devastating consequences of introducing exotic species into native Britain.

LEFT: The elusive and rare bittern, more likely to be heard than seen

TOP: The floating Broads Wildlife Centre on Ranworth Broad

ABOVE, LEFT TO RIGHT: St Benet's Abbey near Ludham; the Swan Inn at Horning; Barton Broad; water-lily flower

EXPLORING THE BROADS

The fine cathedral city of Norwich, on the River Wensum to the west of the Broads, is a good centre for exploring the national park. The foundations of the cathedral were laid in 1096 and it was consecrated in 1101; it is one of the finest Romanesque Gothic buildings in Britain. Norwich Castle, with its Norman foundations, is also worthy of closer inspection and contains the city museum and art gallery.

Among the villages located on the Broads, Wroxham has long been regarded as the capital. Attractively set on the River Bure, which runs right through the heart of the village, it is a centre for boat hire and holidays, and today, with adjacent Hoveton St John, has become a major tourist centre for the Broads.

Ranworth, on the edge of Ranworth Broad, is not to be missed. The view from the tower of the medieval St Helen's Church repays the long climb up and is one of the finest in the Broads. It extends over the gardens of the village to the Malthouse and Ranworth Broads, towards the dark-green carr woodlands of Ranworth Marshes, and the silvery, winding course of the Bure. The church itself – thatched until a fire in 1963 – contains one of the finest and best-preserved painted rood screens in the country and an illuminated songbook, both dating from the 15th century. Nearby is the Broads Wildlife Centre, a Norfolk reed-thatched building which floats on pontoons on the edge of Ranworth Broad, giving superb views of the boat-free water.

There are many wonderful places in the Broads, but perhaps the place where its real spirit can best be captured is the thatched and gabled Edwardian house of How Hill. Situated on the highest point of the national park, a mere 40ft (12m) above the sea, How Hill was built by the Norwich architect Edward Boardman, and now serves as an environmental education centre and nature reserve run by the Broads Authority and the How Hill Trust. The views from the house take in the winding River Ant and the reedbeds of Reedham, Clayrack and Bisley, all watched over by the red-brick tower of the Turf Fen windpump. In the grounds, hidden by willows down by the river, is the little eel catcher's house known as Toad Hole Cottage. You half expect to see Ratty and Mole appear at any minute.

PEAK DISTRICT

The Peak District – the first, one of the most popular and, inevitably, the most pressurised national park in Britain – has two contrasting faces, one White, the other Dark. Each of the 'Twin Peaks' – sharply contrasting yet complementary landscapes – has its own loyal aficionados.

TWIN PEAKS

The predominant geology in the south and central area of the 555 square mile (1,437sq km) park is Carboniferous limestone. It was the pearly-grey colour of this 350-million-year-old, fossil-filled rock that gave it the generic name of the White Peak, which one commentator has described as the softer, more feminine side of the Peak.

The landscape of the White Peak consists of a 1,000ft high (300m) plateau of gently rolling pastureland, split by dramatic, steeply sided dales and threaded by sparkling, clear rivers like the Dove, Manifold, Wye and Lathkill, which mysteriously disappear into underground courses during dry spells.

Over a century ago, the distinguished Victorian author and critic John Ruskin (1819–1900) pronounced: '… the whole gift of the country is in its glens. The wide acreage of field or moor above is wholly without interest; it is only in the clefts of it, and the dingles, that the traveller finds his joy.' No doubt the millions of visitors who annually throng Ruskin's 'dingles' like Dovedale, Monsal Dale and the Manifold valley would agree. Most of these delightful dales can be entered only on foot, unlike the broader, more spacious Yorkshire Dales further north. This gives them an intimacy and peacefulness not found elsewhere, and it makes them a haven for some very rare and beautiful wildlife.

Most of the best of the Peakland dales are now protected as nature reserves, such as the Derbyshire Dales National Nature Reserve, which covers parts of Lathkill, Cressbrook, Monk's, Long and Hay dales. The reserve includes superb examples of all the major wildlife habitats of the White Peak, particularly flower-rich grasslands and ash woodlands. Lime-loving flowers, such as common rock-rose and salad burnet, are abundant here, with up to 45 different species found within a square metre. Rarities, which can be seen in places like Lathkill Dale, Miller's Dale and Chee Dale (all parts of the Derbyshire Dales National Nature Reserve), include Jacob's ladder, spring cinquefoil and Nottingham catchfly.

In spring, visitors can marvel at the breathtaking sight of thousands of early purple orchids and cowslips. Insects are equally diverse, and the south- and west-facing slopes are

LEFT: Curbar Edge above the Derwent valley

home to specialities such as the northern brown argus butterfly and cistus forester moth. Breeding birds include the redstart, wood warbler and pied flycatcher, and the rivers and streams (especially the Lathkill, which flows for its entirety over limestone) are among the purest in the country.

The human history of this area goes back to the first signs of man in Britain and so there is much, much more to the White Peak than Ruskin's glens. Monuments, such as the 5,000-year-old neolithic henge and stone circle of Arbor Low, near Youlgreave, and the scores of 'lows' (burial mounds), which punctuate almost every hilltop on the limestone plateau, bear silent witness to those earliest settlers.

In Saxon times the local tribe was known as the *Pecsaetan*, which simply meant 'the dwellers of the Peak'. The Anglo-Saxon word *peac* could mean any knoll or hill, and the Peak District was known as *Pecsaetna lond*, 'the land of the settlers of the Peak'. The modern meaning of peak has disappointed those who come looking for a Matterhorn or Machapuchare in the Manifold valley. The landforms that predominate in the Peak District are horizontal, rather than vertical.

The timeless stone villages of the White Peak, such as Tideswell, Hartington and the famous 'plague village' of Eyam, remain virtually unchanged, to the delight of modern visitors. They come to admire the folk art of well dressing, which can be seen in various villages throughout the summer months (see panel, page 96). This is thought originally to have been a pagan ceremony,

ABOVE, LEFT TO RIGHT: Arbor Low stone circle; Tideswell, a former lead-mining village

TOP: A rural idyll near Ashford in the Water, Monsal Dale

FIVE FACTS ABOUT THE PEAK

1. First national park in Britain, established in 1951.
2. It is one of the most visited national parks in the world.
3. It is the only British national park to be awarded the Council of Europe's Diploma.
4. Northernmost home of many southern species, such as the hobby and nettle-leaved bellflower.
5. Southernmost home of many northern species, such as the mountain hare and cloudberry.

ABOVE, LEFT TO RIGHT: The view from Mam Tor to Hollins Cross; the hobby, a summer migrant

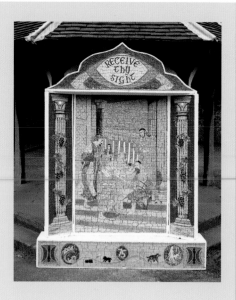

WELL-DRESSED WELLS

The Peak District custom of well dressing is thought to originate from pagan ceremonies of thanksgiving for the precious gift of water, especially on the fast-draining limestone White Peak plateau. The first recorded instance of well dressing was at Tissington in 1758, when the pure water supplies from the village springs were said to have spared the village from the ravages of the Black Death.

Well dressing is a community effort, and many villagers are involved in the process of creating the beautiful dressings. The dressing is designed, usually with a Christian theme, and traced onto paper ready for 'pricking out' in the clay. Next, the villagers scour the surrounding countryside for seeds, flowers, lichens and other natural materials.

The wooden boards that frame the dressing are soaked for several days in a local river or stream to ensure they retain moisture, and then the wet clay is 'puddled', usually by trampling underfoot, to make it pliable and sticky before putting it into the boards, ready to take the petals.

The paper template of the design is then 'pricked out' onto the wet clay, using a sharp instrument, and the design is outlined on the clay using black alder cones, seeds or wool. The real art of a well-dressed well is in the petalling, as villagers press down flower petals, mosses, lichens, grass and rushes to colour in and shade the design.

Finally, the boards are erected near the village well, spring or pump, where they stand for about a week.

giving thanks for the gift of water on the fast-draining limestone plateau. It later became adopted by the Christian church, and now takes place annually in about 40 villages.

More worrying is that the easily accessible limestone of the White Peak, mined since Roman times for its lead ore (see panel, page 104), and the unique semi-precious fluorspar Blue John, is also the most threatened of Peakland landscapes. Huge quarries scar parts of the limestone plateau, especially around the edges of the park at Buxton, Matlock and Ashbourne, hence these fine towns were excluded from the national park when the boundaries were drawn up. Many of these enormous quarries have been in operation since long before the Peak District National Park Authority was able to offer protection. Since then, it has striven to stop quarrying damaging this fragile landscape.

THE DARK PEAK

The more ruggedly masculine Dark Peak occupies the northern part of the Peak District, extending in two enclosing arms down either side of the White Peak, like the remaining hair on the head of a balding man. Before the last Ice Age, the limestone was completely covered by layer upon layer of gritstone, laid down by huge rivers flowing from the north. Then came the crushing power of glaciers and aeons of wind and rain that scoured it all away, exposing, once again, the bare, bleached skeleton of the White Peak beneath.

Abrasive millstone grit (it gets its name from its former use for grinding and millstones) is the predominant rock here, and it outcrops in the Peak's famous gritstone edges, which frown down for many miles on the valley of the Derwent in the east,

TOP: A decorated well at Ashford in the Water
RIGHT: A young mountain hare hiding out on Kinder Scout

ABOVE, LEFT TO RIGHT: Thorpe Cloud, Dovedale; Thor's Cave; a pastoral scene in the Manifold valley

and in the more complex system of cloughs (rocky streams) in the west, where the Roaches in the Staffordshire moorlands offer an equally dramatic serrated skyline when viewed from the west.

The moors above and beyond the edges rise to the high points of Kinder Scout at 2,088ft (636m) and Bleaklow at 2,077ft (633m) – surprisingly, the largest area of land above 2,000ft (610m) in England. These boggy, peat-covered moors are an important carbon sink, and as internationally rare as the rainforest, but are rapidly eroding due to over-grazing and climate change. Urgent measures have been put into place by the National Trust and the Moors for the Future project to try to halt their decline and release of carbon. These have included blocking drainage channels to 're-wet' the peat, the re-seeding of certain areas with heather brashings and the fencing of Kinder Scout and Bleaklow.

The Dark Peak moors are the home of the mountain hare, the ubiquitous red grouse, the curlew and the golden plover, plus raptors such as the merlin and peregrine falcon. They also provide some of the toughest walking in the country, undertaken by a strange and steely, determined breed of walker affectionately and appropriately known as bogtrotters.

THE GREAT ESCAPE

It's been 60-odd years since Professor C. E. M. Joad stated that in his day 'hiking had replaced beer as the shortest cut out of Manchester'. Writing in *The Untutored Townsman's Invasion of the Country* in 1946, he described what he called 'the second industrial revolution', which had enabled townspeople to escape at weekends into the surrounding countryside, particularly the Peak, for recreation. It's still not unusual to see a well-equipped walker kitted out in anorak, breeches and boots striding along Piccadilly in Manchester or Fargate in Sheffield heading towards the railway station and a day out walking in the Peak. Such a figure would almost certainly attract attention if witnessed in, say, London or Bristol. It was the late broadcaster, Council for National Parks president and Peak-lover Brian Redhead who dubbed the park 'The Great Escape'.

TOP SIGHTS

❶ Castleton Show Caves: Peak Cavern, Speedwell Cavern, Blue John Cavern and Treak Cliff Cavern reveal the weird and wonderful underground world of the Peaks.

❷ Chatsworth House and Gardens, near Baslow: magnificent home of the Dukes of Devonshire.

❸ Eyam, near Grindleford: the 'Plague village', with memorials to victims.

❹ Haddon Hall, near Bakewell: fortified medieval manor house, home of the Dukes of Rutland.

❺ Lyme Park (NT), near Stockport: home of the Legh family and backdrop to the immensely popular television production of Jane Austen's novel Pride and Prejudice.

❻ Old House Museum, Bakewell: museum of local life in Bakewell's oldest building.

❼ Padley Chapel, Grindleford: site of the arrest of two Catholic martyrs.

❽ Peveril Castle (EH), Castleton: castle built by William the Conqueror's son.

TOP, LEFT TO RIGHT: *Rock climbing on the Roaches; peat groughs; sheep on the upland plateau of Kinder Scout*   ABOVE: *The Riley graves at Eyam*

ABOVE: *The dramatic gritstone escarpments of the Roaches and Hen Cloud, in the Staffordshire moorlands*

For a 2s 6d (13p) bus ride from their homes in inner-city Manchester, they got out to Hayfield, on the edge of the Peak District moors. Every weekend, they explored the Peak and Whillans told his biographer: 'I thought nothing of thirty miles a day when I'd been at it a bit. I knew the moors like the back of my hand; I knew every funny-shaped tuft of grass, I knew every stretch of peat, I knew every grough, every feature in a radius of twenty miles from Hayfield.' Later, both Brown and Whillans went on to conquer Himalayan mountains such as Kanchenjunga, Annapurna and the Mustagh Tower, using the skills they had honed on Peak District gritstone.

GRAND HOUSES AND ESTATES

The Peak has more to offer, though, than beautiful landscapes and physical challenges. Stately homes such as Chatsworth, Haddon Hall and Lyme Park, on the outskirts of Stockport, show the benign influence of great landowners through their extensive parklands and neat estate villages, providing further major attractions for modern visitors to the park. Minor stately homes include 17th-century Eyam Hall, home of the Wright family for more than 300 years, and Tudor Tissington Hall, seat of the Fitzherberts since the early 1600s.

Many of these manorial estates, including Chatsworth and Haddon, homes of the Dukes of Devonshire and Rutland respectively, occupy the shale valleys carved by the great Peakland rivers like the Derwent and Wye. These broad valleys serve as a kind of transition zone between the Dark and White Peaks, where the landscape is softer and more sylvan, and many fine trees decorate landscaped parklands created with far-sighted vision by men like Capability Brown two centuries ago.

The Peak District has often been compared to an island, surrounded as it is by great industrial cities. But it's an island where the only passport you need is an appreciation of beautiful countryside, and the will to go out and enjoy it.

ABOVE: *The Emperor Fountain at Chatsworth, home of the Devonshires*

YORKSHIRE DALES

There are few English scenes more instantly recognisable than the view looking down on one of the Yorkshire Dales from the windswept heather moorland above. Typical is the scene looking north up Swaledale towards Muker from Hill Top, on the old bridleway above Gun Ing Lane.

WELCOME TO PARADISE

The view from Hill Top shows the old village of Muker, dominated by the tower of its Elizabethan church, seemingly growing organically from the bedrock. The village sits like a spider at the centre of an intricate web of drystone walls spreading up the slopes of Kisdon Hill and Muker Side. Below, in the green dale, every couple of enclosed meadows seems to have its own little gabled barn, ready to take the summer's harvest of sweet-smelling, herb-rich hay.

In the valley bottom, where Straw Beck joins the swirling Swale, clumps of alder trees soften the scene. But high above on the fellsides the native limestone breaks through the surface in the prominent 'scars' of Thwaite Stones and Kisdon Scar. And above all this there is the constant backdrop of the brooding moors, leading up to the lonely, evocatively named summits of Lovely Seat and Great Shunner Fell.

The magnificent Yorkshire Dales inspired that most English of composers Edward Elgar (1857–1934) who, although chiefly associated with his beloved Malvern Hills in Worcestershire, also spent some time in the Dales, staying with his friend Dr Charles Buck at Giggleswick. His glorious melody *Salut d'amour* (formerly *Liebesgruss*) is said to have been composed as an engagement present to his future wife, Caroline Alice, while he was here.

The Dales have also inspired writers. Proud Yorkshireman J. B. Priestley (1894–1984) wrote: 'In all my travels I've never seen a countryside to equal in beauty the Yorkshire Dales'; while local walker and author Alfred J. Brown went even further: 'It is a landscape which brings those prepared to explore it on foot as close to Heaven as you get on Earth.'

In a famous paean to the Dales in his 1928 book, *Four Boon Fellows*, Brown went as far as to write:

> *There must be dales in Paradise,*
> *Which you and I will find,*
> *And walk together dalesman-wise,*
> *And smile (since God is kind)*
> *At all the foreign peoples there*
> *Enchanted by our blessed air!*

LEFT: Muker, the 'capital' of Upper Swaledale

TOP: *Pastoral Wensleydale*

ABOVE, LEFT TO RIGHT: *Late summer near Pateley Bridge; rich grazing land in Swaledale*

SHAPED BY MAN AND ICE

Of all the British national parks, with the possible exception of the Broads, the landscape of the Yorkshire Dales has been most directly influenced by centuries of agriculture and mining. It is a landscape almost entirely shaped by humans over the last 10,000 years since the last Ice Age; from the tidy walled pastures and barns of the dales themselves, to the barren moorlands created partly by deforestation, since when they have been home to generations of nibbling, white-nosed and curly-horned Swaledale sheep. So it's entirely appropriate that the head of a 'Swaddle' tup (or ram) is the symbol of the national park. Only the inaccessible crags (or scars) of limestone, such as the great 300ft (90m) amphitheatre of Malham Cove – once a waterfall even higher than Niagara – or the overhanging monk's cowl of Kilnsey Crag in Wharfedale, could be said to be unaffected by mankind… and even they are the playground of gymnastic rock climbers today.

THE GLORIOUS DALES

The Yorkshire Dales National Park was the seventh to be designated, in 1954, and it covers an area of 683 square miles (1,769sq km) of North Yorkshire, making it the fifth largest in the family. The recently-proposed westward extension of the park, currently undergoing consultation, would increase the area by nearly a quarter or 162 square miles (420sq km), making the total area 842 square miles or 2,182sq km.

The proposed extension brings in the dramatic valley of Mallerstang, threaded by the Settle–Carlisle railway and watched over by the forbidding heights of Wild Boar Fell (2,323ft/708m); the northern Howgill Fells (the southern Howgills are already in the park); the Orton Fells, centred on Great Asby Scar (1,352ft/412m), west of Kirkby Stephen; and the Barbondale and Middleton Fells to the east of Kirkby Lonsdale. The major valleys that make up the Yorkshire Dales are Wharfedale, Malhamdale, Ribblesdale, Dentdale, Wensleydale and Swaledale, most named after the rivers that rush through them, or their major villages. Each dale has its own distinctive character, and many visitors find they have their favourite. For some, it's the stern grandeur and sheer wildness of Swaledale in the far north, with its extensive lead-mining legacy. For others, it's the gentler scenery of

ABOVE: *A misty morning near Hawes*

Wharfedale, dubbed the Queen of the Dales, and punctuated by limestone wonders such as Kilnsey Crag. Many more enjoy the Three Peak Country of Ribblesdale, threaded by the filigree lacework of the impressive 24-arch Ribblehead viaduct, or the pastoral splendours of Wensleydale, with its wonderful waterfalls.

The name of the Swale, in the northernmost of the main Yorkshire Dales, is a bit of a mystery, because unlike most rivers in the Pennines, which have ancient Celtic names, the Swale's originates from the Old English for 'whirling, rushing river' or 'wild one'. This is an accurate description of this boisterous watercourse, notorious for its rapid rises and frequent flooding. The upper reaches of the Swale are said to have the steepest gradient of any major English river – about 1 in 160.

The name of Swaledale's northern tributary of Arkengarthdale is pure Old Scandinavian, meaning 'the valley of Arnkell's enclosure'. Arnkell was a common Scandinavian name, and records show that an Arkil, son of Gospatric, held the estate just

before the Conquest. The dale is known for its strange-sounding place names; Whaw, for example, comes from Old English and means an enclosure for cattle, while the amusing Booze simply means house by the bow, or curve, of the Arkle or Slei Gill Beck.

The main tourist and residential centre of Wharfedale is Grassington, with Kettlewell coming a close second. During the summer their quaint cobbled streets teem with crowds of visitors. There are many remains of lead mining (see panel, page 118) to be seen on the green limestone hillsides surrounding both villages. Further up the dale, at Lea Green, extensive remains of field systems and settlements reveal much earlier human activity, probably dating back to Iron Age and Romano-British times.

Kilnsey Crag, which marks the height of the Ice Age glacier that carved out Wharfedale, also delineates the limit of the white-walled limestone country of Wharfedale. Beyond, the millstone grit giants of Yockenthwaite Moor at 2,109ft (643m) and Buckden

TOP SIGHTS

❶ Aysgarth Falls, Wensleydale: a series of three cascades reached through woodland.

❷ Bolton Abbey, near Skipton: part of the Devonshire Estate, with a ruined monastery.

❸ Bolton Castle, near Redmire, Wensleydale: built by Sir Richard Scrope in the 14th century.

❹ Dales Countryside Museum, Hawes: the story of the Dales.

❺ Hardraw Force, Wensleydale: the highest (100ft/30m) single-drop fall in England.

❻ Ingleborough Cave, Clapdale: perhaps the finest show cave in the Dales.

❼ Malham Tarn: focal point of the stunning limestone area owned by the National Trust.

❽ Middleham Castle, near Leyburn (just outside the park): huge Norman keep.

❾ Thornton Force, Ingleton Glens: at the head of the Ingleton Falls walk.

❿ White Scar Cave, Ingleton: an impressive, well-lit series of caves.

ABOVE: Aysgarth Falls

TOP, LEFT TO RIGHT: Kilnsey Crag; the Blue Bell Inn at Kettlewell; a view of Whernside from Dentdale

Pike at 2,302ft (702m) rear up at the head of the dale, occupying the lands of the ancient hunting forest of Langstrothdale Chase.

Ribblesdale is certainly the wildest and remotest part of the park, and Natural England has designated part of Ingleborough as a 'wilderness zone'. It is dominated by the celebrated Three Peaks of Whernside at 2,414ft (736m), Ingleborough at 2,373ft (723m) and Pen-y-ghent at 2,273ft (693m) – the objects of a popular 26-mile (42km) walk, the Three Peaks Challenge. Ribblesdale also has underground wonders to tempt potholers. Perhaps the most famous sporting caves are Gaping Gill, on the southern slopes of Ingleborough, where Fell Beck drops an awesome 340ft (104m) into the gaping void, and Hull Pot, to the northwest of Pen-y-ghent's noble summit.

This is also the Dales' waterfall country. The gentle 4-mile (6.5km) stroll up the valley of the River Twiss from Ingleton to Thornton Force to see the most powerful waterfall in the Dales, at 45ft (14m) high, should not be missed. The return journey descends into the twin valley of the River Doe and rewards you with another treat – the view of Ingleborough from Twisleton Lane.

Wensleydale – formerly known as Uredale after the river – may not have the grandeur of Ribblesdale or Wharfedale, but it was the favourite of early visitors like John Wesley (1703–91) and Charles Kingsley (1819–75). The stone-built villages, such as Bainbridge and West Burton, some clustering around village greens, all have stories to tell. There's also plenty of history in

Middleham, at the entrance to the dale. This medieval township, watched over by its castle ruins, was the home of Richard, Duke of Gloucester and later King Richard III. Further up the dale is Bolton Castle, the Scrope family's 14th-century stronghold, where Mary, Queen of Scots was detained for a year.

Hawes is a bustling market town at the social and commercial centre of Wensleydale. The old railway station is home to the excellent National Park Centre and informative Dales Countryside Museum. Just across the dale from Hawes is the spectacular waterfall of Hardraw Force, reached through the Green Dragon Inn, which falls uninterrupted for 100ft (30m) in a beautiful little wooded amphitheatre.

The scenic wonders of Malhamdale are well documented and are highlighted by Malham's spectacular cove. This was once a 300ft (90m) waterfall, higher than Niagara. Nearby is the equally dramatic Gordale Scar, where Gordale Beck issues straight from

ABOVE: Limestone pavement below Ingleborough
LEFT: Kisdon Force, stepped falls near the village of Keld

TOP: Early purple orchids

the rock at its heart, and the geological oddity of Malham Tarn, a natural lake in the centre of leaky limestone country.

ON THE ROCKS

Most of the rocks now visible in the Yorkshire Dales date from the Carboniferous period, between 350 and 280 or so million years ago. For much of this time, the Dales were laid down under a shallow subtropical sea in which millions of tiny sea creatures lived. When they died, they slowly sank to the bottom to be consolidated into the underlying sedimentary rock. The lowest of these rocks formed in this way was limestone, named Great Scar limestone because of the huge scars, or cliffs, it formed at the south of the park. This layer is estimated to be about 800ft (245m) thick, giving an idea of the timescale of the deposition.

Hot, mineral-rich water, forced up by heat from the earth's core, left behind veins of lead ore, or galena, which gave the Dales one of its most important industries – lead mining (see panel, page 118). The easily accessible limestone was also highly prized, resulting in huge bites being taken out of the landscape, but quarrying is now regulated by the park planning policies.

Shallow underwater shelves closer to the shores attracted corals and algae to form gigantic reefs, which are more resistant to erosion and have left the conical reef knoll hills of Stebden Hill, Kail Hill and Elbolton, between Thorpe and Cracoe, all in Upper Wharfedale. Later, the limestone was blanketed by spreading deltas of coarse pebbles and grit that flowed down in great rivers from the north, creating layers of shale and sandstone, forming what is known as the Yoredale Series. Later still, towards the end of the Carboniferous period, the highest and final layer was laid down – the dark, weather-resistant gritstone.

The Great Scar limestone dominates the landscape around Malham, Settle and Ingleton, where much of the overlying rock has been stripped away, while the peaks of Ingleborough and Pen-y-ghent owe their shape to the gritstone caps. The smoothly rounded fells of the Howgills, which dominate Sedburgh in the northwestern corner of the national park, are a geological anomaly; they were formed from the same Silurian slates found around Coniston in the southern part of the Lake District. These

440-million-year-old rocks are much older and unlike anything else in the Dales, but make fine walking country.

IT'S ALL IN THE NAME

Many of the place names in the Yorkshire Dales have Norse or Scandinavian roots, a legacy from the Viking, Norwegian and Danish settlers known to have inhabited the area. You can still trace their presence in the Dales with the names they left behind, many of which reflect the importance of landscape features to these early settlers. Old Norse names still common in these hills include 'clint' and 'grike', on the limestone pavements (see panel, page 116); 'beck', the Norse name for a stream; 'seat',

ABOVE: *Pen-y-ghent – one of a trio of hills in Upper Ribblesdale known as the Three Peaks*

THE RAILWAY THAT REFUSED TO DIE

British Rail's axe was poised to fall on the Settle–Carlisle railway, one of the most spectacular rail routes in the country, in the early 1980s, before an extraordinary campaign involving railway enthusiasts, walkers, local people and countryside lovers saved it from extinction.

The Midland Railway built this 72-mile (116km) line in 1875 to carry express and freight trains between Scotland and the Midlands. The line had to be taken through some of the most difficult but beautiful terrain of the Dales, and this was part of its downfall as the 325 bridges, 21 viaducts, 14 tunnels and 20 stations inevitably made it one of the most expensive lines to maintain. It would have been easier just to close it down, but the determined campaigners, who used the magnificent 24-arch Ribbleshead viaduct as their symbol, were determined not to let it go, and their victory in 1989 was one of the great conservation triumphs of the decade.

It is now seen by the National Park Authority as a crucial, green and sustainable tool for getting visitors into the Dales and off the over-crowded roads.

TOP: *The Ribbleshead viaduct, 104ft (32m) high*

WATCH YOUR STEP

Walking on limestone pavements can be hazardous, and it is easy to break or twist an ankle.

The surfaces of these weathered plateaux are characterised by smooth blocks of limestone (known as clints) divided by deep fissures (known as grikes) that have been created by acidic rainwater dissolving the limestone.

The deeper grikes now act as miniature hothouses for plants such as herb robert, hart's tongue fern and stunted juniper or hazel bushes, offering protection from the nibbling teeth of grazing sheep and the withering Yorkshire winds.

Unfortunately, the weird shapes of the clints became a much sought-after feature for garden rockeries and walls, and many acres were stripped away before they were given legal protection in 1981.

Limestone pavements form part of many important Sites of Special Scientific Interest (SSSIs) in Yorkshire, such as the area above Malham Cove, west of Ingleborough at Twisleton and Claphamdale.

TOP: *Gordale Scar, near Malham*
ABOVE: *Grikes divide the clints*

'side' or 'sett' (Old Norse *saetr*) for a summer pasture, as in Appersett and Marsett in Wensleydale; and 'foss' (or force) for a waterfall. The very name 'dale' itself comes from the Old Norse word *dalr*, which translates as 'valley'.

The Norsemen – whose ancient influence can still be seen in the characteristic long-limbed, laconic Dalesman – were not the first settlers in the Dales. The earliest trace of human presence is found in the enigmatic hut circles and field systems that cover large areas of Malham Moor and around Grassington. These possibly originated in the Bronze Age, when the kinder climate meant arable farming was possible on these heights. The most visible and impressive monuments date from the later Iron Age, by which time the climate had deteriorated and people were competing for reduced resources. Earthworks known as hill-forts, were built either for defensive purposes or as summer sheilings from which a watch could be kept over grazing animals.

Ingleborough, the best known of the 'hill-forts', and the highest in the country, may not have fulfilled either purpose. It is now thought that the pear-shaped 15-acre (6ha) earthwork that tops Ingleborough, the 2,372ft (723m) monarch of Ribblesdale, served a purely ritual function and was never inhabited. There is a folk story that it was the site of the last stand by the Celtic king Venutius against the invading Romans, but there is no historic evidence to support this legend of a Yorkshire Masada.

The next invasion was by the Normans, and William the Conqueror's infamous 'harrying of the north' laid waste to large areas of the Dales as he sought revenge against an insurrection, started by the Saxon earls. Edwin, then Edgar Atheling, from the royal line of Wessex, was proclaimed king in York. William acted swiftly to suppress the uprising, instigating a systematic campaign of genocide, which, according to contemporary accounts, left 100,000 dead. One chronicler, Simeon of Durham, tells how the land lay derelict for nine years, and how starving survivors were reduced to eating dogs, and cats and wolves tore at the corpses of the dead. William built imposing castles at Richmond, Skipton and Middleham, and their massive towers still lord it over their towns and the surrounding countryside.

By the Middle Ages, the power of the Church governed large parts of the Yorkshire Dales. Great religious houses, such as Fountains Abbey in Skeldale and Jervaulx in Wensleydale, were granted land by wealthy people and the monks turned the entire area into sheep ranches. The granges, as the outlying farms belonging to the monasteries and abbeys were called, still exist in the shape of modern farms in many of the dales. The monks were also interested in lead – mainly to roof their still beautiful though now ruined abbeys – but the real heyday of lead mining came in the 18th and 19th centuries, when large companies were set up to raise capital and work the elusive veins (see panel, page 118). For many years, Dales people conducted a dual economy of farming and mining.

TOP, LEFT TO RIGHT: Dent Head viaduct; near Green How Hill, west of Pateley Bridge

FLORA AND FAUNA

The great wildlife spectacle of the Yorkshire Dales is to be found in the unfertilised limestone meadows, where a huge variety of wild flowers, including the delicate, pink-flowered bird's-eye primroses, cowslips and pansies, can be found during spring and early summer. Up on the high fells the purple saxifrage is a rare find.

Birdlife is most interesting on the higher moorland areas, where peregrine falcon, hen harrier, merlin and the ubiquitous buzzard can often be seen hunting in search of prey. Golden plover, snipe, curlew and red grouse also use the heather for nesting and feeding, while foxes and badgers haunt the woodlands in the valleys below. The Dales' clean, fast-flowing rivers are home to ring ouzels, dippers and grey wagtails; and recently, and most encouragingly, they have seen the return of otters.

There are only two natural lakes in the Dales – Malham Tarn and Semerwater – but both are of national importance for their aquatic wildlife. The Malham Tarn Field Studies Centre, on the shores of the tarn, is one of the leading environmental research and education centres in the country, and 337 acres (136ha) of the area is now a National Nature Reserve, which is cared for by the National Trust.

TOP: *The ruins of Old Gang Smelt Mill, Swaledale*
RIGHT: *The view over Semerwater*

ABOVE, *LEFT TO RIGHT: Golden plover; foraging badgers*

NORTH YORK MOORS

The North York Moors is a high shoulder of moorland lying midway down the east coast of England, where nature and mankind have combined to create one of Britain's most beautiful and varied landscapes.

A PLACE APART

Thousands of years of human activity have shaped this landscape where, in a single day's walking, you can pass from wild moorland to deep forests and softly wooded dales, rich in wildlife, to a heritage coastline that has provided evidence from the days when dinosaurs ruled the earth. In passing, you could tramp along medieval stone trods or drovers' tracks, encounter some of the finest monastic remains in the country, and see evidence of a once intensely worked industrial landscape.

Few places in Britain can match the variety of the North York Moors, and few are as accessible, whether you use the 1,438 miles (2,314km) of rights of way in the national park (a third of which is now classified as open country under the Countryside and Rights of Way Act), or the extensive network of riding and cycling routes, which include the 110-mile (176km) Moor to Sea cycle route between Pickering and Great Ayton and the mountain-biking mecca of the Forestry Commission's Dalby Forest in the south of the park.

Alternatively, the park is also very well served by public transport, with the Moorsbus Network operating throughout the summer months. This provides a convenient, relaxed, car-free and carefree way of enjoying the best of the national park, without the worry of road congestion and parking and with the added bonus of knowing that you are doing your bit to conserve this precious environment.

The North York Moors is also the driest of the national parks, the high tops receiving only 45in (1,143mm) and lower altitudes only 30in (762mm) of rain annually. This is because the prevailing winds in Britain are normally from the southwest, so much of the rain falls on the neighbouring Pennines, effectively putting the North York Moors in their rain shadow.

In summer, the high moorland of the park is covered in a purple sea of rolling heather – the finest display of this hardy moorland plant in the country (see panel, page 122). You can see this wonderful sight on Farndale, Rosedale or Westerdale Moors, or

LEFT: Looking north towards the distinctive outcrop of Roseberry Topping

HEATHER MOORLAND

One of the great glories of the North York Moors National Park is its heather moorland: in late summer, it has been estimated that there are as many as 3,000 million flowers to the square mile.

The moorland, which covers more than 170 square miles (44,000ha) of the park, is an important wildlife habitat and is therefore awarded special protection. The land is also managed and used by farmers and gamekeepers for sheep grazing and the rearing of red grouse. The birds are raised for the lucrative shooting season, which runs from the 'Glorious Twelfth' of August to 10 December.

Heather has a lifespan of 20 to 30 years and can reach a height of 2–3ft (just under a metre) if left to its own devices, but farmers burn small, carefully controlled areas of old heather over winter and in early spring to allow the new shoots so beloved of grouse and sheep to come through.

Although when viewed from a distance it may seem that the vast acres of colourful heather are a monoculture of a single plant, that is far from being the case.

The most common species of heather is ling, with tiny pink flowers appearing from mid- to late August, but there are also colonies of bell heather (recognisable by its deeper-purple flower) on drier, steeper ground, and the related cross-leaved heath (with its larger, rose-pink flowers) in the wetter patches. All make delicious honey, and hives on the moors are a common sight.

ABOVE: *Typical heather moorland above Fryupdale*

from any of the cross-moorland roads, such as the A171 Whitby to Scarborough road, or the minor road over Blakey Rigg, between Hutton-le-Hole and Castleton.

Heather moorland (see panel, opposite) covers 35 per cent of the total area of the national park, and when photographed by satellite appears as a bottle-green mass extending in an arc from the Vale of York to the North Sea coast.

This moorland is one of the great glories of the 554 square mile (1,434sq km) North York Moors National Park, and one of the main reasons for its designation as the sixth in the series in 1952. Moreover, there are few landscapes in the British Isles that are so precisely defined by their natural boundaries as the North York Moors. To the motorist heading north on the A1 trunk road, or the rail traveller journeying north of York on the East Coast main line, the moorlands form a constant, misty-blue outline away to the east – mysterious uplands that always seem apart and aloof.

A SHATTERED DOME

The geology of the North York Moors is relatively simple to understand, and it could be said that the science of geology started here, in the shape of William Smith. Smith, who lived at Hackness, drew the first geological map of Britain, published in 1815. The story of 'Strata' Smith and the North York Moors' geology is told in Scarborough's Rotunda Museum, opened in 1829 and recently the subject of a £4.4 million restoration. The moors' geology is based on sedimentary rocks laid down in a shallow sea during the Jurassic period some 150 million years ago, which were then uplifted by enormous subterranean forces about 70 million years ago into a broad dome, known to geologists as the Cleveland Dome.

This landform dominates the northern and western sandstone moorlands of the national park and has been planed off by further marine submersion, Ice Age glaciers and aeons of wind and rain into a broad, undulating plateau.

The dome has been split by the deep valleys of a series of south-flowing rivers, which rise on the moorland above, and in the north by the eastward-flowing Esk. The rivers of the southern

TOP: *Red grouse*

TOP SIGHTS

❶ Byland Abbey (EH), near the village of Wass: 13th-century abbey ruins.

❷ Helmsley Castle (EH), Helmsley: ruins of the late 12th-century castle built by Walter Espec.

❸ Hole of Horcum: a huge natural amphitheatre on the A169 Pickering–Whitby road.

❹ The Moors National Park Centre, near Danby: a perfect introduction to the park and a great day out whatever the weather.

❺ North Yorkshire Moors Railway: steam railway running between Pickering and Whitby.

❻ Rievaulx Abbey (EH), near Helmsley: impressive monastic ruins in Ryedale.

❼ Ryedale Folk Museum, Hutton-le-Hole: open-air museum with historic buildings.

❽ Whitby Abbey (EH) and Visitor Centre, Whitby: atmospheric clifftop ruins.

LYKE WAKE WALK

Local farmer Bill Cowley was probably responsible for more blisters than any other person in the country. In 1955, he came up with the idea of a 40-mile (64km) walk, which crossed the highest points of the North York Moors between Osmotherley and Ravenscar. And what's more, to become a member of his Lyke Wake Club, you had to complete the moorland marathon inside 24 hours.

The name of the walk is taken from an ancient folk song called the Cleveland Lyke Wake Dirge (hence members are known as 'dirgers'). This rather mournful ditty was originally sung over the bodies of the dead and depicted the imagined journey of their souls across the bleak moors after death. 'Lyke' is the Norse name for a corpse and 'wake' is the watch kept over it.

The exhausting route became so popular with walkers, particularly those raising money for charity, during the 1960s and 70s that severe erosion on parts of the route resulted in it spreading to more than 100 yards (92m) wide in places and damaging the delicate habitat of the peat and heather moorland.

However, in recent years the popularity of the walk has declined, and with so many alternative walks in the area, and the programme of path restoration undertaken by the Park Authority, the Lyke Wake Walk has recovered much of its original character.

dales all eventually flow into the Yorkshire Derwent and then into the mighty Humber. The shorter northern dales all join the Esk to enter the sea at Whitby.

All these river valleys have been broadened and deepened by the action of Ice Age glaciers, and nearly all have the characteristic U shape associated with the grinding, eroding power of ice. There are few waterfalls in the North York Moors National Park, but the one at Mallyan Spout, near Goathland, a 70ft high (21m) cascade of water reached by a rocky path, can easily rival those of the neighbouring Yorkshire Dales National Park (see pages 106–119).

To the south and west of the park, the dominant rock of the Hambleton and Tabular Hills is oolitic limestone, giving a softer, lower landscape, which sometimes looks a bit more like the Cotswolds than northern England. The steep western escarpment of the Hambleton Hills at places like Sutton Bank, however, provides one of the finest views in the north of England – across the vales of Mowbray and York towards the distant Pennines and Yorkshire Dales.

The sedimentary rocks of the North York Moors are relatively short of minerals, although ironstone was mined extensively in Rosedale, where the massive stone arches of the 19th-century kilns look like the ruins of some ancient Mayan temple, stranded out on the moors.

LEFT: Helmsley Castle
TOP: Danby Dale from Castleton Rigg

ABOVE: Forge valley, near Scarborough

Minerals were also mined on the spectacular 26-mile (42km) coastal strip of the national park, which includes the highest cliffs on the east coast (Boulby Cliffs, near Staithes, are 660ft/201m above the sea). Alum for the textile industry was mined from the shale near Sandsend.

Potash and rock salt are still being mined in what is claimed to be the deepest mine shaft in Europe on the cliffs at Boulby, where the unseen mine extends 2 miles (3.2km) under the North Sea. The mine is also an underground laboratory for research into dark matter, a building block of the universe.

ALONG THE COAST

The glorious coastline is followed by the 109-mile (176km) route of the rollercoaster Cleveland Way National Trail, which includes geological highlights such as the concentric rocky curves of the wave-cut platform at Robin Hood's Bay, revealed at low tide. Looking like the layers of skin on an onion, the platform has been eroded by the constant battering of the North Sea, and is a great place to seek out fossils and their living crustacean counterparts.

The section of coastline between Saltburn in the north and Scalby Ness, near Scarborough in the south, was classified in 1974 as the North Yorkshire and Cleveland Heritage Coast. The cliffs and beaches are rich in the fossils of marine animals that flourished in the tropical seas and estuaries of the Jurassic period 150 to 185 million years ago.

Palaeontologists' finds have included giant reptiles, such as the 40ft long (12m) long-necked plesiosaur (the model for the Loch Ness monster), and ichthyosaurs, which looked more like

TOP: Robin Hood's Bay from Stoupe Brow, Ravenscar

ABOVE, LEFT TO RIGHT: St Hilda's Abbey at Whitby; Whitby harbour

ABOVE, LEFT TO RIGHT: Boulby Cliffs, the highest cliffs on the east coast of England; the beach at Runswick; the village of Robin Hood's Bay

modern fish but had a row of sharp teeth. A number of dinosaur footprints have also been discovered on the sandstones between Ravenscar and Scalby Ness and the alternative name for the Heritage Coast is the Dinosaur Coast.

Much more common are ammonites, an astonishingly successful animal with a spiral, coiled shell. According to a local legend, they were formed when St Hilda, the Abbess of Whitby, cast a spell over a plague of snakes that had infested the coastline. The snakes were driven over the cliffs, then coiled up and petrified to form what were known locally as snakestones. Some were even given a snake's head, to make them appear more realistic, and modern science gave a nod to the legend when it named some local species of ammonites *Hildoceras* after St Hilda.

Other fossils found along the Heritage Coast include the shell-like brachiopods; belemnites, known locally as the Devil's thunderbolts but actually a distant relative of squids; crinoids, looking like sea lilies; and spiral-shaped gastropods, ancestors of snails and winkles. You should not remove fossils from the cliffs, but there are usually plenty of examples to be found scattered among the rock debris on the beach. Always check the tide tables before you start your exploration.

The North Sea coast of the North York Moors is not only subject to never-ending erosion by waves, it is also often blanketed by an all-pervading mist locally known as a 'roak'. These roaks, also known further north as sea fret, can be seen moving slowly in from the sea until they envelop everything in their clammy dampness.

LEFT: The headland at Kettleness from the Cleveland Way
ABOVE: Staithes harbour

DAFFODILS AND DROVERS

One of the highlights of the year in the North York Moors is the glorious springtime display of wild daffodils that can be seen in Farndale, north of Kirkbymoorside.

Other floral highlights – apart from the heather on the high moors (see panel, page 122) – include a range of rare orchids found in the limestone meadows on the southern edge of the park. These meadows run in a belt 30 miles (48km) wide stretching from Sutton Bank in the west to Hackness Hill, near Scarborough, in the east of the park. The orchids have been encouraged by agricultural conservation schemes instituted by the national park.

Birdlife on the high moors is dominated by the red grouse, usually classified as a subspecies of the continental willow grouse. Curlew, lapwing, golden plover and snipe all also breed among the heather, and the dashing, thrush-sized merlin hunts in low-flying sweeps across the ground.

The most prominent features of the moors, however, are the 20 to 30 wayside crosses that have been used for centuries to guide travellers across this daunting terrain. Most date from the medieval period and may have been erected by the moors' ruling monastic community (see panel, opposite).

A few have been given names, some of which are as colourful as the heather in which they stand. We are left to wonder who Ralph, of Old and Young Ralph Cross (which provides the symbol of the national park), white-painted Fat Betty and Margery were.

One of the most important routes that crossed the western part of the North York Moors was the Hambleton Drove Road, which crossed the Hambleton Hills on an ancient ridgeway between Swainby and Sutton Bank. This was part of a highway that linked the south of England and Scotland, and was used to transport Scottish cattle to markets in the south during the 18th and 19th centuries. Scottish drovers usually purchased their animals – often Galloway or West Highland cattle – from farmers, and then drove them across country to the lucrative markets in Malton, York and London.

ABOVE: Daffodil time in Farndale

THE MONASTIC LIFE

The North York Moors have attracted spiritual and religious communities for many centuries. Writing in the 12th century, St Aelred, third abbot of Rievaulx in Ryedale, situated on the wooded banks of the Rye on the edge of the moors, recorded that he had found there 'peace, everywhere serenity, and a marvellous freedom from the tumult of the world'.

Now in stately ruins, Rievaulx was the first Cistercian foundation in Yorkshire and dates from 1132. It is thought by many people to be the most beautiful of England's monastic ruins. The abbey became the mother church of the order, and fitted the white-robed Cistercian's need to escape from the 'tumult of the world' perfectly. At its height, the abbey housed 140 monks and employed another 240 lay brothers and 260 hired workers, who looked after their 14,000 sheep on the vast sheep ranches that extended over the moors.

Another Cistercian house on the edge of the moors, near the village of Wass, is Byland Abbey. The monks arrived here in 1177 and built the impressive, 26ft diameter (8m) circular west window – it was unfortunately shattered during the Reformation a few years later. It remains the largest abbey nave in the country, and was the largest of all the Cistercian houses. Byland is renowned for its magnificent medieval tiled floors.

TOP: *The splendid ruins of Rievaulx Abbey*

ABOVE, LEFT TO RIGHT: *The Danby Show; the Millennium Cross erected by the North York Moors Association at Rosedale Head*

TOP: *Hutton-le-Hole, a showpiece village where two becks meet*

In the mid-18th century, over 30,000 Scottish cattle crossed into England every year, and the trade gradually increased during the following century. During this time about 75,000 animals were sold annually at Smithfield Market in London, many coming from Scotland. Vast flocks of sheep and lesser numbers of pigs, geese and turkeys also used the route.

The local communities generally welcomed drovers because they would bring the latest news and also act as a postal service, delivering letters. The men either camped out at night or stayed at wayside inns such as Spout House, in nearby Bilsdale. This started life in the 16th century as a thatched farm cottage and later became an alehouse known as the Sun Inn. The cruck-framed, stonewalled house had fallen into disrepair when the National Park Authority acquired it in 1979, but it was re-thatched and now stands in all its former glory.

A much more recent landmark on the moors is the truncated pyramid of the Fylingdales Early Warning Station (which replaced the white 'golf balls'), designed to warn of approaching nuclear attack. This alien-looking structure is now used as part of the USA's Missile Defence System.

TOP SPOTS

One of the best places from which to explore the moors is Helmsley. This is the 'capital' of the park, with a picturesque market place and cross and late 12th-century castle built by Walter Espec, whose keep-like east tower dominates the town. The castle did not see action until the Civil War, when it endured a three-month siege by Parliamentarian forces before being starved into submission in 1644. The Black Swan Hotel, which incorporates a 16th-century half-timbered house, overlooks the busy cobbled market square, where a street market is held every Friday. On the edge of town is the fine early 18th-century mansion known as Duncombe Park, which succeeded the castle as the home of the lord of the manor in 1713.

Among the other attractive settlements of the North York Moors is the showpiece village of Hutton-le-Hole, with its velvety, neatly cut village green enclosed with white-painted railings. Hutton is the home of the Ryedale Folk Museum, one of Yorkshire's leading open-air museums, which tells the life of the moors through 4,000 years.

Nearby, at Lastingham, lying in a fold of the moors, is St Mary's parish church. It was built in the 11th century on the site of a Celtic monastery and is famous for its superb vaulted crypt. Reached via stone steps, the crypt is unique in England in being like a little church in its own right, with two side aisles and an apse. Services are held here regularly.

However, the Moors National Park Centre is one of the best introductions to the park, with its comprehensive range of information and lively exhibitions and displays.

TOP: Approaching Goathland Station

LAKE DISTRICT

The Lake District, tucked away in the northwest of England, is often described in tourist literature as 'the most beautiful corner of England'. It can also be said with some justification to be the birthplace of the international notion of national parks.

WHERE IT ALL BEGAN

This sublimely lovely district inspired local poet William Wordsworth (1770–1850) to write one of the first tourist guides to the area – *Guide to the Lakes*, published in 1810. In the conclusion he famously hoped that he might be joined 'by persons of good taste throughout the whole island, who, by their visits (often repeated) to the Lakes in the North of England, testify that they deem the district a sort of national property, in which every man has a right and interest who has an eye to perceive and a heart to enjoy'.

We had to wait another 141 years for this 'national property' to be realised, but in 1951 the Lake District became the second national park in Britain. It covers 885 square miles (2,292sq km) and is the largest and one of the most popular parks in England. The recently announced eastward extension of the park, covering the fells around Borrowdale including Whinfell Beacon (1,621ft/494m) between the A6 and the M6, would increase the area of the park by three per cent (28 square miles/73sq km), to 911 square miles/2360sq km. The extension would effectively link the Lakes to the Yorkshire Dales National Park, the boundary being marked by the deep Lune valley containing the roaring traffic of the M6.

Several Lakeland views are familiar to people who have not even visited the park. For example, the view up Wasdale towards Great Gable was recently voted the nation's favourite view. Coincidentally, it was also the scene chosen by the Lake District National Park Authority as the basis for its logo.

It was Wordsworth who came up with an analogy that neatly explains the topography of the Lakes. He asked his readers to imagine themselves on a high point, such as Great Gable or Scafell (or wandering in a cloud hanging above them), and see 'stretched out at our feet a number of valleys, not fewer than eight, diverging from the point on which we are supposed to stand, like spokes from the nave of a wheel'.

Readers were also invited to picture the scene before the arrival of man: 'He may see or hear in fancy the winds sweeping over the lakes, or piping with a loud voice among the mountain peaks; and, lastly, may think of the primeval woods shedding and

LEFT: Derwent Water, a centre for sailing, canoeing and windsurfing

A LITERARY LANDSCAPE

During the Romantic Age of the early 19th century, the Lake District became synonymous with some of the finest English poetry. William Wordsworth, born and brought up in Cockermouth, led the Lakeland School.

Many of his poems, like his autobiographical Prelude (1799), were inspired by the Lake District landscape. He collaborated closely with his beloved sister, Dorothy, when they lived at Dove Cottage, Grasmere, which is now a museum and memorial to his works, cared for by the National Trust.

Working with Samuel Taylor Coleridge and Robert Southey, Wordsworth developed a new, more accessible style of poetry, which became very popular in the 19th century and will be forever linked to the Lake District. Wordsworth and Coleridge were close friends, and Coleridge moved to Greta Hall at Keswick in 1800 to be near him. He married the sister-in-law of Robert Southey, who also moved to Greta Hall in 1803, and became Poet Laureate in 1813, to be succeeded by his mentor, Wordsworth, on his death in 1843.

A third poet of the Romantic Movement, Thomas de Quincey, joined the Wordsworth circle after he had visited them at Dove Cottage; when William and Dorothy moved to Rydal Mount, Grasmere, he took over the lease of the cottage. Other visitors included John Keats, Sir Walter Scott and Charles Dickens.

Coming after the Wordsworth coterie, art critic, author and early conservationist John Ruskin moved to Brantwood, on the eastern shore of Coniston Water, in 1871. His house is open to the public.

TOP: *View across Coniston Water to the Old Man*

STONE TO SLATE

The first settlers in the Lake District were probably neolithic hunter-gatherers, but on the whole their transient, nomadic existence left little trace. However, a series of industrial sites on some of the highest fells provides evidence of their fleeting presence. A look at the Ordnance Survey map covering Langdale will reveal the words 'Stone Axe Factory' on the steep slopes below Pike o' Stickle, showing where the greenish-grey volcanic tuff rocks were excavated and then turned out as axes more than 4,000 years ago.

The beautifully shaped stone implements represented the height of Stone Age technology, and were finished and polished down on the coast, later to be exported all over Britain through a surprisingly sophisticated trading system. Other 'factories' have

since been discovered at Mickledore, on the way to Scafell Pike, and on the rocky little peak of Glaramara at the head of Borrowdale. Lake District axes have been found as far away as East Anglia and the south coast of England, showing that there was a highly developed market.

But the most obvious and striking remains of prehistoric man in the national park are the mysterious, evocative and superbly sited stone circles at places like Castlerigg, above Keswick, and on the slopes of Black Combe on the southernmost edge of the fells at Swinside. The Romans also left their indelible mark on the Lake District in the forts they constructed to guard key routes through the forbidding fells. Hardknott Fort, the best preserved, is perched at the summit of the Hardknott Pass on a shelf under the crags of Border End, commanding extensive

ABOVE: About 40 stones make up the stunning circle at Castlerigg

views down to the lush, green lowlands of the Esk Valley. Clear evidence that the Vikings occupied the Lakeland fells is found, as elsewhere, in the place names of the national park. The invaders bequeathed the names of thwaites (clearings), fells (hillside with open grazing), tarns (small mountain lakes) and becks (brooks or streams). Steeper ravines take the Old Norse name of gill or ghyll, while waterfalls are called fosses, again from the Old Norse. We even know the names of some of these early Norse settlers, because they are preserved in place names, such as Ennerdale (Anund's valley), Windermere (Vinandr's lake), Haweswater (Hafr's lake) and Seat Sandal (Sandulf's sheiling).

The major settlements of the Lake District – Kendal and Keswick – are situated on the southern and northern approaches respectively. Kendal, famous for its high-energy delicacy, Kendal Mint Cake, houses the interesting Museum of Lakeland Life and Industry, and in the town park are the ruins of the castle in which Catherine Parr, sixth and final wife of Henry VIII, was born.

Keswick became the home of another Lakeland industry after plumbago or graphite – locally known as wad – was discovered at Seathwaite and the famous Lakeland and Cumberland pencil industry was founded. Copper was also mined extensively in the Coppermines valley in the shadow of Coniston Old Man, and the green Lakeland slate was excavated from quarries at Coniston, Honister and Langdale.

The main villages and tourist centres within the national park boundary are Coniston, the twin settlements of Bowness and Windermere, Ambleside and Grasmere.

NORTHUMBERLAND

There are few places left in England where you can gaze across great vistas of beautiful and uninhabited countryside with just the sounds of nature for company. Officially designated as the country's most tranquil place, the Northumberland National Park fulfils this promise with room to spare.

LAND OF FAR HORIZONS

Northumberland National Park consists of 404 square miles (1,048sq km) of rolling moors and picturesque valleys, stretching from the Hadrian's Wall World Heritage Site in the south to the Cheviot Hills and the Scottish border in the north.

The valleys of the national park run mostly west to east, where crystal-clear salmon rivers chatter around isolated, stone-built villages and ancient hay meadows. Each dale nurtures a rich culture of traditional music and folk tales, rooted in the lawless days of the medieval Border outlaws (known as reivers) and in the struggles of hill farming in remote places.

Hill country is Northumberland's speciality. The distinctive, volcanic Cheviot Hills harbour an Iron Age hill-fort on almost every summit, and the valleys beneath have picturesque names such as the College, the Breamish, the Harthope and the Coquet.

Upper Coquetdale has a secret history of illicit whisky distilling and trading across the border. Downstream, near the market town of Rothbury, the meandering river sweeps around the dark sandstone ridge of Simonside, with great Bronze Age burial cairns perched along its crest, and spectacular examples of prehistoric rock art at its foot.

Striding out along the highest part of the Hadrian's Wall National Trail between Walltown and Chesters, with its steep northern-facing cliff and southern slopes full of meadow flowers and heather, you can follow the Roman auxiliary's gaze from 2,000 years ago. This extended out to the supply fort at Vindolanda and the high fells of the North Pennines to the south, or north across the empty, rain-soaked, lough-spattered wilderness, where the lurking, ever-present threat came from the barbarian Caledonians.

It took only eight years, an astonishingly short time, to build Hadrian's Wall (see panel, page 151). Fifteen miles (24km) of some of its best-preserved sections, its milecastles and forts, form the southern boundary of the Northumberland National Park. Hadrian's surveyors knew exactly how to make the most of the natural features in the landscape when they built his wall. They utilised the natural defence formed by the igneous outcrop

LEFT: Dove Crag in the Simonside Hills

known as the Great Whin Sill, which runs west to east across the south of what is now the national park for much of the central section of the wall. Here it runs along a switchback, rolling ridge, with the vertical crags of the Whin Sill exposed and forming a natural barrier to the north.

The Whin Sill, created when molten rock was forced through vertical fissures from the depths of the earth, forms one of the most striking physical features in the north of England. It not only provides the foundations for the most spectacular sections of Hadrian's Wall, it is also responsible for the waterfalls of High Force and High Cup Nick in the Durham Pennines, and it outcrops again at the Northumbrian coast, where it forms the foundation for the castles of Bamburgh, Dunstanburgh and Lindisfarne. The isolated, seabird-haunted skerries of the Farne Islands are the final, seaward extension of the Whin Sill.

A PARK OF TWO HALVES

Northumberland National Park was the ninth to be designated, in 1956. It has often been described as England's Empty Quarter, and with only 2,200 permanent residents within its boundaries, it is certainly the most sparsely populated and one of the least

visited of all our national parks. Paradoxically, it is the very sense of isolation and wildness that is one of its most attractive features for the 2.4 million visitors who come here annually to enjoy the peace, solitude and wide views.

Northumberland is a national park of two halves, and in fact was originally proposed by John Dower in 1945 as two separate parks, which he named the Roman Wall and the North East Cheviots. The area between the high ground of the Cheviot Hills and the wall has been altered by the timber industry and water demand. The enormous forest of Kielder – the largest in Europe – and the huge, 2,684-acre (1,086ha) Kielder Water reservoir, are both excluded from the park. They are, nevertheless, very popular with visitors who don't mind their landscapes man-made.

The other great man-made feature in the park between the wall and the Cheviots is the 59,600-acre (24,120ha) NATO Otterburn Live Firing Training Area, which covers a fifth of the area of the national park between Redesdale and the valley of the Coquet. The army has been encamped at Otterburn since 1911, but it still comes as a bit of a surprise to learn that when the red flags are flying you cannot walk there. But in recent years, in

TOP: Climbing on the Whin Sill of Steel Rigg, west of Housesteads

HADRIAN'S WALL

Hadrian's Wall was built at the behest of Emperor Hadrian between AD120 and 128 to mark the northernmost limit of his empire, and as a barrier against the possible invasion by the Caledonians from what we now know as Scotland.

Current thinking is that the wall served a dual purpose – for defence and as a political border. It is a masterpiece of military engineering, and one of the finest examples of Roman military architecture anywhere in Europe, still impressive after nearly 2,000 years. It is amazing to think that it took the force of 10,000 professional legionaries (not slaves, incidentally) only eight years to complete, with its series of turrets, milecastles, forts and the vallum – a sort of no-man's-land between the wall and the military road, which paralleled it to the south. The wall ran for 80 Roman miles (73 miles/117km) across the neck of England from the Tyne to the Solway.

The Roman engineers cleverly utilised the outcrop of volcanic Whin Sill rock for much of the wall's length, placing it on top of the cliffs and giving it a natural defence against attack from the north. Hadrian's Wall is now a UNESCO World Heritage Site, and in the care of English Heritage.

TOP: View of the wall, looking towards Sycamore Gap

TABLETS OF TIME

In 1973, archaeologist Robin Birley unearthed scraps of wood from a wet drainage pit at the settlement of Vindolanda, south of the wall. On them he discovered faint scratchings made by a Roman pen (or stylus).

Vindolanda writing tablets are still being found today and most are now kept in the British Museum in London.

Years of excavation, restoration and interpretation have revealed much about what life was like for the soldiers and their families nearly 2,000 years ago: from what they ate and drank and what they wore, to what they thought of some of their senior colleagues and their own family and friends.

The messages were written in ink on so-called 'leaf' tablets, made of imported spruce or larch. These were preserved because the anaerobic conditions in the drainage pit prevented them from rotting.

Other messages are known to have been written onto reusable beeswax-covered tablets, but unfortunately most of these tablets have perished.

An on-site museum tells the story of Vindolanda, south of Housesteads.

---

conjunction with the national park, Defence Estates have made a positive effort to encourage public access to the Otterburn Ranges. A website, www.otterburnranges.co.uk, now provides an interactive map, information and a number of downloadable walks describing the historical remains and wildlife that can be seen. This includes the rare black grouse, which is making a significant comeback on the ranges thanks to efforts by conservationists to improve the birds' habitat.

The Simonside Hills and Harbottle Hills, southeast of the Otterburn Training Area and stretching between the fortified village of Elsdon and the market town of Rothbury, are more Pennine in their character than the granite summits of the Cheviots further north. Their heather-topped escarpments are reminiscent of a Peak District edge, and many of the sandstone boulders that litter their bases were used by prehistoric man to peck out many enigmatic 'cup-and-ring' markings (see panel, page 160).

The best place to see these markings is at Lordenshaws, south of Rothbury, where there is a whole series of earth-fast, flat-topped boulders in the shadow of an Iron Age hill-fort. These have been used to carve out concentric rings, spirals, cups and interlinking channels. No one is exactly sure what these intricate examples of what is now known as rock art meant to their carvers, but they are thought to date from the neolithic (New Stone Age) period, about 5,000 years ago. Other impressive examples can be seen at Roughting Linn, near Ford.

THE FINAL CHALLENGE

The view north from the Simonside escarpment above Lordenshaws extends across the broad, patchwork-quilt landscape of the Coquet valley towards the distant blue outline of the Cheviot Hills, the highest ground in the national park.

The Cheviots are the final great challenge on Tom Stephenson's marathon up the backbone of England – the Pennine Way. They represent some of the toughest walking to be found on the 270-mile (434km) national trail. The reason for this lies in their geology; the Cheviots represent the eroded remains of a great granite boss formed when a huge volcano, situated just to the west of the 2,676ft (815m) summit of the reigning peak of the Cheviot, spewed out its lava about 300 million years ago. Several thousands of feet thick, the lava gives the pinkish hue to the grey granites, which are rarely exposed but can be seen in places such as the Hen Hole and the Schil in the remote College valley.

One of the characteristic features of the Cheviots and a hazard for walkers on this stretch of the route is the overlying cloying, ankle-sucking peat bog. However, the National Park Authority has laid down sandstone-flagged paths through many of the most difficult stretches of mire along the way – to prevent walkers from eroding this important and sensitive habitat, as well as making the route safer. In addition to providing a home for wading birds, the peat bogs have a flora including some of Britain's rarest plants, such as sundew, bog asphodel, bog rosemary and dwarf cornel.

TOP: Remains of the Roman fort at Vindolanda, near Bardon Mill

RIGHT: Kielder Water – Europe's largest man-made lake – and Forest Park

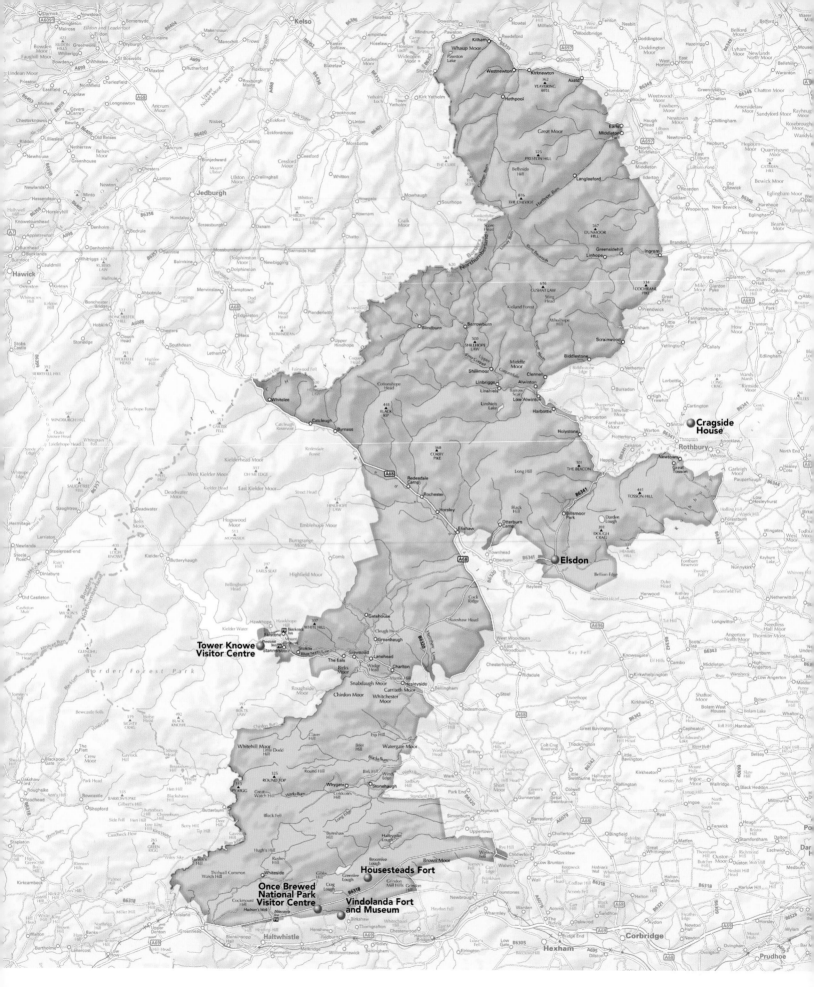

WATERFALLS AND WILDLIFE

Although spectacular waterfalls in the Northumberland National Park are few and far between, there are two in particular worth visiting. One is Linhope Spout, a 60ft (18m) water chute near the village of Linhope in the foothills of the Cheviot Hills. Dippers, grey wagtails and oystercatchers are familiar sights here on the Linhope Burn, a tributary of the River Breamish.

Further south, Hareshaw Linn, near Bellingham, just north of Hadrian's Wall, is another. The water (linn is an old name for a waterfall) cascades obliquely for 33ft (10m) across a rock face at the head of a wooded, 100ft high (30m) canyon. The waterfall is reached by a path, first constructed in Victorian times, that criss-crosses the stream over several attractive bridges. Rare ferns, mosses and lichens thrive in the gorge, which has been designated a Site of Special Scientific Interest because of the diversity of its wildlife.

The Cheviots are sheep country par excellence (home of the white-faced breed of the same name), and the tawny moor grass of their smooth-sided slopes is known locally as 'the White Country' in contrast to the dark, heather-clad moors of the Simonside and Harbottle Hills to the south and east, called 'the Black Country'. The high peat moorland of the Cheviots may seem to be a wildlife desert, but in fact it is the home of a variety of birds and animals.

Most typical perhaps is the curlew, frequently heard on the high moors in summer, its call seeming to epitomise the wild spirit of these lonely heights. Conservationist and ornithologist Peter Scott (1909–89) wrote: 'The sight and sound of a curlew can bring the national park to life and turn our thoughts to the real meaning of conservation.' So it was appropriate that the silhouette of an alighting curlew was chosen to be the emblem of the national park in 1957.

TOP SIGHTS

❶ Cragside House (NT), near Rothbury: former home of industrialist Lord Armstrong.

❷ Elsdon: village, church and pele tower.

❸ Housesteads Fort and Museum (EH): best-known and best-preserved fort on Hadrian's Wall.

❹ Once Brewed National Park Visitor Centre, near Bardon Mill: close to Hadrian's Wall and the park's main visitor centre.

❺ Tower Knowe Visitor Centre, Kielder Water: overlooks the dam that forms Kielder Water, with exhibitions of the history of the area.

❻ Vindolanda Fort and Museum, near Bardon Mill: excavated buildings and a good museum.

ABOVE, LEFT TO RIGHT: Cragside, the first house in the world to be lit by hydroelectricity; the hypocaust under the granary at Housesteads Fort

TOP, LEFT TO RIGHT: Fungi; curlew, the largest of the British waders; Hareshaw Linn waterfall

ABOVE: Hotbank Farm, with the line of Hadrian's Wall, Crag Lough and Highshield Crag in the background

REIVERS AND PELE TOWERS

At the height of the Border conflicts, it's said that when the lady of the house was short of meat, she would present her lord with a spur on a plate – the sign that it was time he saddled up, donned his 'steel bonnet' and stole some more cattle.

It's hard to believe today, but the now silent hills of Northumberland once echoed to the sound of warfare as family battled against family, clan against clan, for 300 or so years. These were the times when the troubled border between England and Scotland was known as 'the debatable land', and cattle stealing and internecine strife were the order of the day. These dark deeds were recorded for posterity in the famed Border Ballads collected by Sir Walter Scott.

It was also when well-to-do families built four-square pele (pronounced 'peel') towers onto their manor houses, where they could shelter in times of siege. Good examples can be seen at Elsdon and Alnham. Many other farms were fortified with massively thick stone walls and tiny slit windows, and were known as bastle houses.

TOP: Elsdon pele tower in Elsdon, the park's largest settlement

The raptors that haunt these wild places include red kite, hen harrier, merlin, buzzard and raven, while typical mammals include hare, fox, badger and, making a welcome comeback in the fast-flowing clean river valleys, the elusive otter.

CASTLES IN THE AIR

Apart from the mysterious rock art carvings (see panel, page 160), the other major prehistoric feature of the hills of the Northumberland National Park is the hill-forts. One look at the Ordnance Survey map of the Cheviots will reveal the telltale Gothic lettering that signifies prehistoric 'castles in the air'. There are estimated to be about 50 hill-forts in the national park, most dating from the Iron Age (about 2,000 years ago).

The name was given to them in Victorian times, but modern archaeologists are not so keen on emphasising the predominantly military or defensive use for these hilltop structures. They were probably built as much to overawe neighbouring rival tribes, or as summer sheilings from where their herds of livestock could be watched.

Some of the most impressive of Northumberland's hill-forts are found in the Cheviots, and the College valley is ringed by beautifully preserved examples such as Great and Little Hetha, Ring Chesters and North Blackhaggs. Nearby and looking north towards Scotland are the very impressive Yeavering Bell and Humbleton Hill, on whose slopes the Border Battle of Homildon Hill was fought in 1402. Yeavering Bell is particularly interesting. It is the largest hill-fort in Northumberland, covering 13 acres (5ha), and contains the foundations of about 130 round houses. It stands inside a massive stone rampart on a twin-topped, dome-like hill overlooking the valley of the River Glen. In its shadow are the remains, excavated in 1977, of Ad Gefrin, the wooden palace of the Anglian king Aethelfrith, where St Paulinus baptised Aethelfrith's son, Edwin, into the Christian faith in AD627.

According to the Venerable Bede (c673–735) in his *Ecclesiastical History of the English People*, 'the people… gathered from all the surrounding villages and countryside; and when he (Paulinus) had instructed them, he washed them in the cleansing waters… in the nearby River Glen'. It is fascinating to imagine the scene as local people, farmers and shepherds gathered together from the surrounding countryside under the shadow of Yeavering Bell, where their ancestors had probably worshipped heathen gods, to learn of the new religion.

Interestingly, both Ad Gefrin and Yeavering translate as 'the hill of the goats', and the Cheviots are still the home of several herds of feral goats that were reintroduced to these hills in the 19th century from Welsh stock. When the palace of Aethelfrith was excavated, the remains of a tall man were found buried beneath its threshold; at his feet lay the skull of a goat.

BORDERS AND BATTLES

This Border country has been the scene of conflict for many centuries, particularly during the times of the reivers during the 15th and 16th centuries (see panel, opposite). But the Border wars had been going on for a long time before that. Place names on the modern map still give chilling reminders of the area's violent and bloody past. Names like Bloodybush Edge, Ogre Hill, Hungry Law and Deadwater Fell are all redolent of that troubled past. Many of these bitter encounters were recorded

ABOVE, LEFT TO RIGHT: Black grouse; detail on a stone pillar from the Mithraic temple at Carrawburgh; feral goat

ROCK ART

Northumberland has the finest collection of prehistoric cup-and-ring marked rocks in Britain. Their foremost discoverer, recorder and interpreter is the retired local school teacher Stan Beckensall, who is internationally renowned for his work on ancient rock art.

There have been many theories about what exactly these intricate patterns of cups, concentric rings, channels and spirals might represent: suggestions range from messages from outer space to ancient representations of the landscape, but no one can be really sure.

They always seem to be carved on prominent rocks overlooking wide areas of countryside, so the latest theory from Beckensall and other archaeologists is that they may have carried some kind of message about the landscape and what it meant perhaps as much as 5,000 years ago.

Some of the best places to see rock art and cup-and-ring marks in Northumberland are Lordenshaws, near Rothbury, Roughting Linn, near Ford, on the Iron Age hill-fort at Old Berwick and on Weetwood Moor, near Wooler.

in the traditional folk songs known as the Border Ballads, a large number of which were collected by Sir Walter Scott (1771–1832) under the title *The Minstrelsy of the Scottish Border*, first published in 1802–03.

One of the oldest, most vivid and oft-repeated of the Border Ballads is that concerning the Battle of Otterburn, which took place in 1388 on the very ground still occupied by the army on the A696 near the village of the same name in Redesdale. It was fought by moonlight on the night of 5 August 1388. James, 2nd Earl of Douglas, had embarked on a violent campaign of destruction and plunder, which had taken him across the disputed border as far as Durham. As he returned north he laid siege to the city of Newcastle-upon-Tyne, where Sir Henry Percy, the eldest son of the Duke of Northumberland and nicknamed 'Hotspur', had taken command of the garrison.

However, the powerful garrison held out against the marauding Scots, and Douglas retreated to Otterburn for the night. Some of his party wanted to return home across the border to Scotland, but Douglas, mindful of Percy's vow that he would not allow the Scottish forces to leave with his pennant, which had been seized, decided he would call Percy's bluff.

The English forces, some 9,000 strong, led by Percy, discovered where Douglas was camped and set off hotfoot for Otterburn, where the Scots were waiting for them. According to the old ballad, Douglas had a fateful dream that night:

But I hae dream'd a dreary dream,
Beyond the Isle of Skye;
I saw a dead man win a fight,
And I think that man was I.

When the battle was joined, on ground north of the A696 to the west of Otterburn (now marked by a monument), Douglas's 'dreary dream' was fulfilled. Although the Scots were outnumbered by three to one they easily overcame the English forces of Percy, who was captured along with his brother, Ralph. The English had lost about 1,800 men with a further 1,000 wounded, and the Scots, although victorious and with far fewer casualties, lost their beloved leader, the Earl of Douglas, whose body was taken home to be buried in Melrose Abbey.

The ballad concludes:
This deed was done at Otterburn,
About the breaking of the day;
Earl Douglas was buried at the braken bush,
And the Percy led captive away.

The distinguished local historian and national park supporter Professor G. M. Trevelyan probably summed up the spirit of Northumberland as well as anyone in his book *The Middle Marches*. He wrote: 'In Northumberland alone, both heaven and earth are seen, we walk all day on long ridges, high enough to give far views of moor and valley, and the sense of solitude below. It is the land of far horizons…'

TOP: *Cup-and-ring carvings on Weetwood Moor, near Wooler*

RIGHT: *Otters are shy and you are lucky if you see one, but they thrive in Northumberland's clean waters*

PEMBROKESHIRE COAST

The salty tang of the sea and the screaming cries of seabirds are almost always present in the Pembrokeshire Coast National Park, because nowhere is more than 10 miles (16km) – and most places are within about 2 miles (3.2km) – from the coast.

A BREATH OF HEAVEN

Pembrokeshire is the only national park in Britain located predominantly on the coast. Its glorious coastline extends over 260 miles (418km), with more than 50 sparklingly clean beaches. It is one of the smallest national parks, covering just 240 square miles (621sq km), and is also one of the most densely populated, with around 23,000 residents – a number that is multiplied more than 600 times by the arrival of an estimated 13.5 million visitors every year.

Pembrokeshire thrusts its fingers out into the storm-wracked Celtic sea; the last windswept western outpost of Wales. Conversely, it was also the first landfall for many invaders throughout much of its history, from the Norsemen who named so many of its physical features to the last, unsuccessful invasion of these islands at Carregwastad Point, near Fishguard, in 1797 by the French. This farcical 'landing' was actually a diversion timed with a rebellion in Ireland, which went disastrously wrong. The motley army of about 1,400 French convicts and

mercenaries, commanded by the Irish-American General William Tate, were probably drunk when they landed. They tried to set fire to the church but were contained by the Pembroke militia and a band of villagers. The village leader was a local cobbler, Jemima Nicholas, who is said to have captured 14 French soldiers on her own. She is buried in St Mary's churchyard.

'LAND OF MYSTERY AND ENCHANTMENT'

There are few places in Britain to which a description coined a thousand years ago can be applied today. The anonymous compilers of *The Mabinogion*, a collection of medieval Welsh folk tales and legends, wrote about Pembrokeshire as *gwlad hud a lledrith* – 'a land of mystery and enchantment', words which have seldom, if ever, been bettered.

Giraldus Cambrensis (c1146–1223), the Welshman born to Norman parents at Manorbier Castle on the south coast, provided another glowing description of his homeland in his *Itinerary through Wales* in 1188. 'Penbroch' (Pembroke), he

LEFT: Porth Clais near St David's

THE PEMBROKESHIRE COAST PATH

The task of surveying the route of the 186-mile (299km) Pembrokeshire Coast Path, which was designed to follow the coast as closely as possible, was entrusted to local author and naturalist Ronald Lockley in 1953.

The long-awaited opening on 16 May 1970 followed 17 years of negotiations and construction of the path, which needed more than 100 footbridges, 479 stiles and many thousands of steps on the steeper slopes. The broadcaster Wynford Vaughan Thomas, then President of the Council for the Protection of Rural Wales, officially opened the trail, claiming that walkers were now able to enjoy 'the most beautiful coast in Britain'.

The National Park Authority publishes 10 pocket-sized guides to sections of the Coast Path, as well as a handy mileage chart for walkers.

TOP AND ABOVE: *The Pembrokeshire Coast Path*

ABOVE, LEFT TO RIGHT: Gannets, Europe's largest breeding seabird;
Whitesands Bay, where the sand really is white; nearing Ramsey Island

TOP: Sunset behind Gateholm Island from Marloes beach

plummets in a vertical, 100ft (30m) power-dive into a shoal of fish, folding its 6ft wide (1.8m) wings back into a lethal arrow at the very moment of impact.

The mysterious storm petrel used to be known by sailors as Mother Carey's chicken, after a fabled witch of the high seas, and this insignificant little bird was a particular favourite of Ronald Lockley. He wrote: 'I have a great affection for this little bird which is no bigger than a sparrow and yet can ride out the endless hurricanes of the Atlantic winter.' There were about 1,000 breeding pairs of storm petrels on Skokholm in Lockley's time. They spend most of their days out at sea feeding close to the surface, apparently 'walking' on the water like little St Peters – hence their name.

Other birds that inhabit Skokholm and the cliffs include the chough, a master of the swirling air currents that sweep up against the cliffs, and its larger, croaking cousin, the raven.

Much more common are the similar, reptilian-looking cormorants and shags. Some of the tiniest and most improbable ledges are occupied by razorbills – a penguin-like, large, black-and-white member of the auk family. It also provides the National Park Authority with its logo.

Razorbills are commonly seen on the Elegug Stacks near the spectacular natural flying buttress of the Green Bridge of Wales on the Castlemartin peninsula. Here, they share their precarious home with colonies of guillemots, fulmars, shags and kittiwakes, and their evocative cries echo constantly around the storm-battered cliffs.

In addition to the grey seals (see panel, below), the other sea mammal you are most likely to see off the coast of Pembrokeshire is the common porpoise, and, less often, dolphins. The impressive sight of a basking shark – one of the world's largest fish – can be the reward of a boat trip to the

CELTIC CREATURES

The Pembrokeshire Coast is home to some of the largest breeding colonies of grey seals in Britain. It's not uncommon to see the inquisitive, bobbing, Roman-nosed head of a seal watching you as you walk along the coastal path, and the sight of the pure white pups on the beaches of Ramsey, Skomer or any other sheltered and inaccessible cove is guaranteed to attract attention.

The first of the liquid-eyed pups are born in August at the height of the tourist season, and as pupping continues into September, the barking of adult females will often be heard along the coastal path.

The mother's milk of the grey seal is extremely rich and nutritious, and the pups double their birth weight within 18 days. After that, they are on their own and tagging has shown that they may swim as far away as Ireland, Brittany or Spain within months of their birth.

From late autumn through to mid-March, many adults and immature seals come back to the Pembrokeshire beaches to moult, when groups of up to 200 have been recorded on Skomer. Paradoxically, much less common is the smaller common or harbour seal, which is half the size of the grey, and has a much less dog-like face.

ABOVE: A grey seal on Caldey Island
TOP, LEFT TO RIGHT: Choughs; Strumble Head lighthouse

RIGHT: The Green Bridge of Wales on the Castlemartin cliffs

islands in summer. More recently, sightings have increased of the strange, disc-like sunfish – usually about the size of a dustbin lid – which spends the greater part of its life feeding on jellyfish in the deep ocean.

The largest land mammals found in the Pembrokeshire Coast National Park are foxes and badgers. There are not thought to be any significant populations of deer in the park, but the shy and elusive otter now breeds along the quiet river valleys of the Gwaun and Nevern.

AN ANCIENT BOUNDARY

Despite its peaceful appearance today, the history of Pembrokeshire is one of conflict and war. The Normans imposed castles on the landscape to intimidate the native people. Moreover, the line of castles, which stretches from Brandy Brook near Newgale in the west to Amroth in the east, effectively split the county into two – a cultural division still recognisable today and marked by an invisible line known as the *Landsker*.

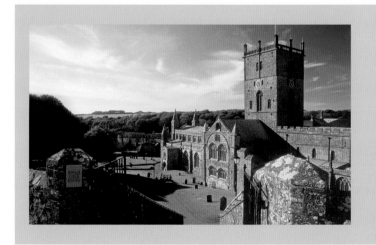

The land north of the *Landsker* (a Norse term meaning a boundary) is still sometimes known as 'the Welshry', and the churches and chapels have a very Welsh look; the language and place names are Welsh. Coastal headlands and estuaries have the Welsh prefixes of 'pen' and 'aber'. Meanwhile, to the south of the *Landsker*, in the area once known as the 'Englishry' or 'Little England beyond Wales', the settlement names are generally English-sounding, and the churches have typically

TOP: St Bride's Haven

ABOVE: St David's Cathedral

OFFA'S DYKE NATIONAL TRAIL

The 177-mile (285km) Offa's Dyke National Trail has been described as 'not the oldest, nor the longest, but the best' of Britain's many and varied long-distance walking routes.

It follows the line of the massive earthwork built by Offa, ruler of the Midland kingdom of Mercia, in the 8th century to mark the boundary between his land and Wales. Even as late as the 10th century, Saxon law stated that 'neither shall a Welshman cross into English land nor an Englishman cross into Welsh land without the appointed man from the other land who should meet up with him at the bank and bring him back from that other land without any offence being committed'.

In the Brecon Beacons National Park, Offa's 'bank' traverses the ridge above the Vale of Ewyas towards Hay Bluff, with splendid views on all sides.

ABOVE: *Offa's Dyke National Trail, officially opened in 1971 by Everest hero Lord John Hunt, who lived at nearby Llanfair Waterdine*

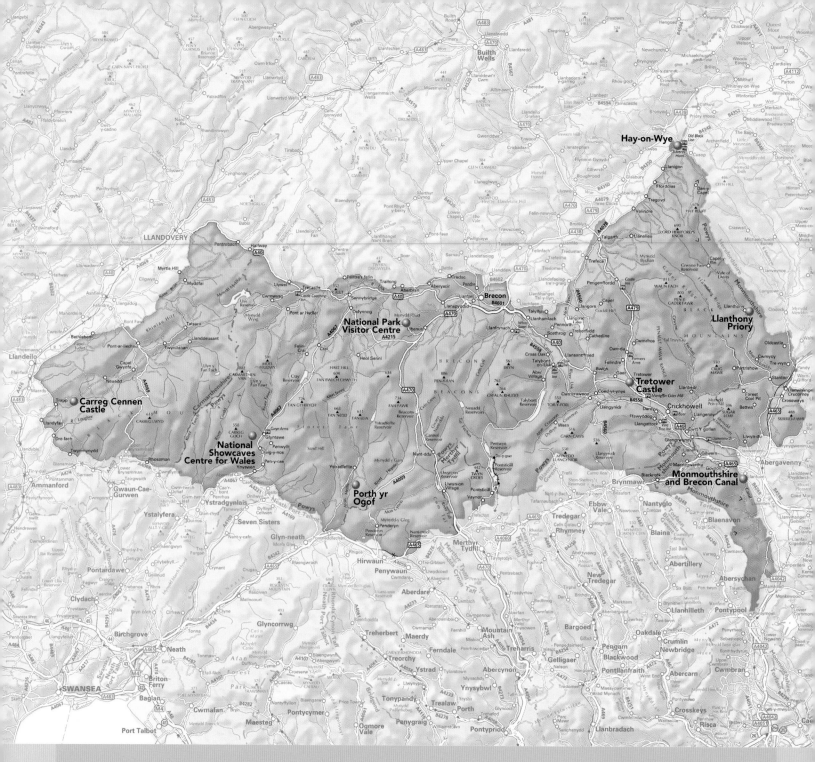

TOP SIGHTS

1 Carreg Cennen Castle, near Llandeilo: the most spectacularly sited of the park's castles.

2 Hay-on-Wye: small town that has become known for its second-hand bookshops.

3 Llanthony Priory, Vale of Ewyas: ruins of a 12th-century monastic retreat east of the Black Mountains.

4 Monmouthshire and Brecon Canal: the only canal lying entirely within a British national park.

5 National Park Visitor Centre, near Libanus: on the moorland slopes of Mynydd Illtyd.

6 National Showcaves Centre for Wales, Dan yr Ogof in the Tawe valley: three splendid caves plus other attractions, and a fascinating museum that tells the story of limestone.

7 Porth yr Ogof cave entrance, in the valley of the Mellte: one of the largest cave entrances in Britain, approached by a steep and tricky footpath. Visitors should not go inside the cave.

8 Tretower Castle, near Crickhowell: a castle-within-a-castle, with a medieval manor house close by.

LITTLE TOMMY JONES

A simple, rugged obelisk on the Craig Cwm Llwch ridge below Pen-y-Fan in the Central Beacons serves as a chilling reminder that, despite their modest height, the Brecon Beacons must always be treated with the utmost respect.

Five-year-old Tommy Jones and his father from the mining town of Maerdy at the head of the Rhondda valley had been visiting his grandparents who lived in the isolated farm of Cwm-llwch beneath Pen-y-Fan in August 1900. Night was falling as they walked up from Brecon and little Tommy became separated from his father and wandered off.

A massive search was launched and the story made national headlines, prompting one newspaper to offer a then-sizeable reward of £20 for news of his whereabouts. Tragically, Tommy wasn't found until a month later when a Brecon couple came across his body 2,250ft (685m) up on the exposed ridge. His inquest returned a verdict of death from exhaustion and exposure.

Above the village of Bethlehem, the twin Iron Age hill-forts of mighty Garn (or Carn) Goch – Y Gaer Fawr and Y Gaer Fach – tell of more troubled times when defence was obviously important to the local communities. The ruins of the spectacular 12th-century crag-top castle of Carreg Cennen dominate the lovely Cennen valley near Llandeilo in much the same way.

The Black Mountain is a remote and often mist-wreathed landscape, which seems to have encouraged the creation of myths and legends. One of these is centred on the mysterious Llyn y Fan Fach. The story goes that one day a local farmer from the nearby hamlet of Llanddeusant took his flock of sheep up to the lake. As he sat by the shore, a beautiful girl emerged from the dark waters.

The couple promptly fell in love, but the mysterious girl said she would only be able to marry the farmer if her father consented to the match. So it was arranged that the next time the farmer went up to the lake his sweetheart would appear with her father and her four identical sisters. The father told the farmer he could have his beloved and as many cattle and sheep as he could count, provided he picked out the right daughter.

This was achieved by the girl wriggling her toe when the farmer came up to her, and the marriage was agreed on the condition that if he should ever strike her three times with iron, she would return to the lake, taking her dowry with her. After several years of happy marriage the taboo was broken, albeit accidentally, and the fairy woman did indeed return to the lake, taking the sheep and cattle with her.

However, that was not the end of the story because the couple had five sons, to whom their fairy mother imparted the mystical secrets of healing. The sons, known as the Physicians of Myddfai, became famous all over Wales and started a line of doctors and herbal healers that lasted for over six centuries. The last known Physician of Myddfai, Dr C. Rice Williams, died in 1842 at Aberystwyth.

TOP: The Tommy Jones memorial on Pen-y-Fan
LEFT: Tretower Castle

ABOVE, LEFT TO RIGHT: The path up to Craig Cerrig-gleisiad in Fforest Fawr; A pair of Welsh sheep; looking down on Talybont reservoir

Occupying the whole of the western half of the national park is the Fforest Fawr Geopark, which became a member of the European Geoparks Network in 2005, in recognition of its geological heritage, and a UNESCO Global Geopark in 2006. The Fforest Fawr Geopark is one of only 30 in Europe and the only one in Wales. The designation requires that the National Park Authority and partners work together to conserve the unique geological heritage of the area through integrated and sustainable development, such as the Waun-Fignen-Felin project. Here, the national park has worked in association with local commoners and taken gorse and bracken, cut and crushed from Pen-y-Crug and Mynydd Illtyd Commons, to help restore the seriously degraded peat bog above the Dan yr Ogof cave system, as well as the caves themselves. The mulch has been used to block water run-off channels and thus 're-wet' the 50-acre (20ha) bog.

THE BLACK MOUNTAINS

The Black Mountains (plural) to the east of Brecon form a natural boundary between England and Wales and were used by King Offa to form part of his famous Dyke – now a 177-mile (285km) national trail (see panel, page 181) – during the troubled days of the Dark Ages. The chief town serving the Black Mountains is Abergavenny (Y Fenni), which is dominated by the isolated, thimble-shaped hills known as Blorenge, the Sugar Loaf and Ysgyryd Fawr. This country is more tightly folded and heavily populated than its Carmarthenshire cousin, and accommodates numerous reservoirs, natural woodlands and conifer plantations.

The River Wye (Afon Gwy) parallels the northwest boundary of the national park, which reaches its northernmost limit at the second-hand book capital of Britain, Hay-on-Wye (see panel, below). Dominated by the remains of its 11th-century castle, Hay is an important agricultural centre and its former cheese and butter markets are remembered in the names of its bookshop-lined streets.

Further west, the village of Llangynidr has both the Monmouthshire and Brecon Canal and the River Usk running through it. The five locks on the canal to the west of the village lift the canal 50ft (15.2m) in 0.75 miles (1.2km) around the slopes of Tor y Foel, and form an attractive feature. The River Usk runs on a rocky bed through rapids here, and is renowned for its excellent trout and salmon fishing. Llangynidr bridge, an ancient monument, leads into the village from the A40 to the north. Nearby attractions include the conifer-fringed Talybont Reservoir and Tretower Court and Castle historic house – a fortified manor house and the remains of a Norman castle.

Romantic Llanthony Priory, the ruin of an Augustinian retreat dating back to the 12th century, is sheltered in the remote Vale of Ewyas in the Honddu valley north of Abergavenny. The ruins have a pointed arcade of Early English-style arches, which frame the Black Mountains beyond. The priory was rebuilt from the remains of a modest 6th-century hermitage under the orders of Hugh de Lacy in 1175. Walter Savage Landor (1775–1864), the English writer and poet, was attracted by the peace and

TOWN OF BOOKS

Bookworms swarm to Hay-on-Wye like honeybees round a hive. The bustling little market town, situated picturesquely on the River Wye, at the northern tip of the national park, is a book lovers' paradise. Every other shop seems to have racks of second-hand books both outside and in, and even the former town cinema has been turned into a massive, two-storey emporium of the written word.

Eccentric local entrepreneur Richard Booth of Hay Castle, who at one time tried to make a case for

unilateral declaration of independence (UDI) for Hay from the rest of the UK, started selling second-hand books here in the 1970s. Since then the enterprise has grown enormously, giving the little market town an unexpectedly cosmopolitan atmosphere.

A spin-off for the self-styled 'Town of Books' has been the internationally renowned annual Hay Festival of Literature, which is held every spring. Top authors from all over the world descend on Hay to give readings and take part in lively discussions.

LEFT: The ridges of the Black Mountains on the eastern boundary of the park

ABOVE: One of Hay's many shops for bibliophiles

tranquillity of the place and purchased the site in 1807. By this time some of the buildings had been converted to domestic use by former owner Colonel Mark Wood, and Wood's house now incorporates the small Abbey Hotel. The rest of the ruins are in the care of Cadw. The 13th-century church, which is dedicated to St David, also remains.

Reed-fringed Llangorse Lake (Llyn Syfaddan), the largest natural lake in South Wales, lies between the Black Mountains and Brecon and supports a wide range of wildlife in its extensive reedbeds, swamps and marshy grasslands. This includes the great crested grebe, pochard and goosander, while the thick reedbeds are home to sedge and reed warblers, reed buntings,

ABOVE: Pink sails on Llangorse Lake

and large flocks of roosting starlings. The shy otter, white-clawed crayfish and the blood-sucking medicinal leech – not found anywhere else in the national park – frequent the quieter reaches of Llangorse Lake, which is one of the park's most important Sites of Special Scientific Interest (SSSIs). Another is the National Nature Reserve of Craig Cerrig-gleisiad, just off the A470 north of the Storey Arms, which occupies a huge hollow bitten out of the flanks of Fan Frynych by an Ice Age glacier. Arctic and alpine plants flourish among the rocks, and buzzards and ravens soar overhead. Flowers include the yellow-flowered roseroot and clusters of purple saxifrage, alongside 'lowland' species such as primrose, cowslip and early purple orchid.

WATERFALL COUNTRY

The fourth element that makes up the Brecon Beacons National Park landscape is the belt of Carboniferous limestone and gritstone country lying to the south. Characterised by gorges, waterfalls and caves, the scenery is similar to parts of the Yorkshire Dales.

South of Ystradfellte, the valleys of the Mellte, Hepste, Fechan and Pyrddin rivers show the best of these features. In the valley of the Mellte there is a delightful series of falls easily accessed on foot. Their names vividly convey the descriptive poetry of the Welsh language: Sgwd Clun-Gwyn, or Upper Fall, means 'waterfall of the white meadow'; Sgwd Isaf Clun-Gwyn, like a miniature Niagara, is the 'lower white meadow fall'; and Sgwd y Pannwr is the 'waterfall of the fuller' (or 'cloth washer').

The steep-sided gorges containing the waterfalls were carved out by rushing water 10,000 years ago towards the end of the last Ice Age, when huge volumes of sediment-laden meltwater sought the quickest way to the sea far to the south. The shady environment created by these narrow valleys and overhanging trees encourages rare ferns to grow, seemingly from every crack in the rocky sides, while verdant green mosses, lichens and liverworts blanket almost every exposed rock and tree.

Beneath this delightful area a mysterious subterranean world exists, where some of the most challenging and deepest caving routes in Britain extend far beneath the surface. However, if you prefer to experience these underground wonders safely, then visit the National Showcaves Centre for Wales at Dan yr Ogof in the Tawe valley.

The Brecon Beacons National Park is exceptionally well served by public transport, including the popular Beacons Bus, so it's easy to explore these fascinating and ever-changing landscapes on foot. The National Park Visitor Centre (Mountain Centre), with its wonderful views of the Beacons on the moorland slopes of Mynydd Illtyd near Libanus, provides a stimulating introduction to the park and its varied natural and man-made features, and makes a great starting point for any exploration.

TOP: Canoeist at Sgwd Clun-Gwyn

RIGHT: The Sgwd yr Eira (Spout of Snow) waterfall near Ystradfellte

SNOWDONIA

No one can be absolutely sure what *Eryri* – the Welsh name for Snowdonia, that ruggedly mountainous corner of North Wales containing the highest ground in the British Isles south of Scotland – really means.

PLACE OF EAGLES

The traditional translation of the name suggests that it comes from the Welsh *eryr* meaning eagle, and therefore may mean 'the land of eagles'. However, that romantic (and sadly no longer true) derivation has been questioned in recent years. The fact is that many seemingly obvious literal derivations from the Welsh language are not necessarily the correct ones, and it is now thought that the name is more likely to have come from the medieval Welsh word *eryr*, simply meaning 'a high place'.

No one can deny that Snowdonia is indeed a high place, as this land of mountains contains some of the most spectacular, as well as the highest, British mountain scenery south of Scotland. Centred on its grandest, highest and best-known mountain – 3,560ft high (1,085m) Snowdon (Yr Wyddfa: the 'monument' or 'tumulus' in Welsh) – Snowdonia's intoxicating mix of airy ridges and isolated mountain summits, dramatic ice-carved *cwmoedd* (mountain hollows) and secret, hidden *llynoedd* (lakes), long whaleback ridges and vast open moorlands is an irresistible magnet for all hill lovers, walkers and climbers. However, don't be misled by thinking that Snowdonia is just about mountains.

One of its most fascinating facets for the hill walker is that from many of the rocky summits, you can look down to see the sunlight shining on the shimmering waters of the Irish Sea to the west or the Menai Strait to the north. It's not always appreciated that the national park has 23 miles (37km) of glorious coastline with estuaries, family-friendly beaches, sand dunes and great sweeping bays.

After you have explored the mountains and the magnificent coastal scenery, you can still find yet another, sharply contrasting, landscape in the gentle rivers such as the Llugwy, the Eden and the Dulas, which dash thrillingly through beautiful wooded valleys, punctuated by spectacular waterfalls. The most famous are probably the Swallow Falls (or Rhaeadr Ewynnol – 'the foamy rapids') near Betws-y-Coed, and the Aber Falls on the Afon Llafar beneath the Carneddau range. Snowdonia really does have something for everyone.

Such was its undeniable beauty, Snowdonia National Park – Parc Cenedlaethol Eryri in Welsh – was in the first group to be designated in 1951, and covers 840 square miles (2,176sq km)

LEFT: View from the summit of Snowdon across to Crib Goch (left) and Moel Siabod, in the distance

TOP: Barmouth Sands in Cardigan Bay

ABOVE, LEFT TO RIGHT: The Snowdon Horseshoe from Llyn Mymbyr; mountain goat

Idris was apparently a poet, astronomer and philosopher, and when he was not throwing stones at his rival he liked nothing better than studying the stars from his rocky observatory. All that remains of this legendary chap is the curse of Cadair, which says that anyone careless enough to fall asleep on the summit on New Year's Eve will awake either as a madman or a poet.

Cadair is one of the most popular of Snowdonia's mountains, and it has been well loved by climbers for many years. The ascent from the Idris Gates by Tal y Llyn via the tremendous, ice-scalloped hollow of Cwm Cau and over the riven face of Craig Cau passes through what has been described as one of the wildest mountain scenes in the whole of Wales, and it is certainly one of the finest excursions in the country.

SNOWDON'S SUMMIT

However, the highlight of Snowdonia's mountain fastnesses has to be the Snowdon range itself – jagged peaks which brush the sky and shine like polished armour after the not infrequent rainstorms that lash these bristling heights. No wonder they have become the playground of serious rock climbers.

The analogy with armour is not inappropriate, because the legendary 'Once and Future King' Arthur is said to have fought his final battle with his traitorous nephew, Mordred, on the long saddle between the reigning summit of Yr Wyddfa and Lliwedd. It is still known as Bwlch-y-Saethau – or 'the pass of the arrows' – and Arthur is said to be waiting with his sleeping knights in a cave on the precipitous face of Lliwedd, ready to come to the nation's aid in time of peril.

Snowdon's shapely summit is actually the lowest point of a syncline (or downfold) in the Ordovician rocks, showing the enormous uplifting of the land that has gone on since these rocks were laid down around 500 million years ago. It seems strange that you might find a fossilised Ordovician seashell here on the highest point of England and Wales, but such has been the power of the cataclysmic changes wrought by the various earth movements.

Over half a million people walk on Snowdon every year, of which an estimated 355,000 people reach the summit (once famously described by the Prince of Wales as 'the highest slum in Europe'). There was no doubt that the run-down café just below the summit, built as Robert's Hotel in 1850, had certainly seen better days.

Thankfully, this is not the case any longer, as the National Park Authority, the Welsh Assembly, the Wales Tourist Board and the Snowdon Mountain Railway have pooled resources for the building of a new, £8 million café and visitor centre. As the result of a public vote, the futuristic glass- and granite-walled building was named Hafod Eryri – or 'the summer residence of Eryri' – when it opened in 2009.

Hafod Eryri is a more fitting reward for those thousands of people who, either by rail or on foot via the seven major routes, make it to the summit for the stupendous view which prompted an 18th-century traveller to exclaim: 'It is doubted whether there is another circular prospect so extensive in any part of the terraqueous globe.'

TOP, LEFT TO RIGHT: Llanberis Station; the rare Snowdon lily, which grows on ledges inaccessible to sheep

ROUTES TO THE TOP

Some of the most popular routes up Snowdon start from Pen-y-Pass, the highest point of the Llanberis Pass between the Snowdon massif and the Glyderau. There is a large car park run by the National Park Authority opposite the former Gorphwysfa Hotel, now the 80-bed Pen-y-Pass Youth Hostel. The Gorphwysfa Hotel was the headquarters for many of the pioneering Victorian and Edwardian climbers who first explored these crags, including such notable names as Geoffrey Winthrop Young (1876–1958) and George Mallory (1886–1924), the young climber who disappeared on the northeast ridge of Everest in 1924, either in the final stage of his attempt to reach the summit, or after having been the first to reach it.

One of the best scenic routes to Snowdon's summit is the so-called Pyg Track, which leads up from Pen-y-Pass. It is said to have got its name from the Pen-y-Gwryd Hotel, which stands at the foot of the Llanberis Pass at the junction of the Beddgelert to Capel Curig and Llanberis roads. The Pen-y-Gwryd is as famous

as Pen-y-Pass in the world of climbing, because it provided the base for the successful 1953 Commonwealth Everest expedition. Here they did much of their training and the testing of their oxygen sets, which were to prove so crucial to Edmund Hillary's (1919–2008) and Sherpa Tenzing Norgay's (1914–86) famous ascent of Everest.

Snowdon was chosen because, albeit on a much smaller scale, it bears more than a passing resemblance to the topography of Everest. The Everest Room at the Pen-y-Gwryd is filled with historic memorabilia of the expedition, including the signatures of most of the members of the expedition – written, perversely, on the ceiling!

The Pyg Track leads up to Bwlch y Moch, which means 'the pass of the pigs', so this may be where the name came from. However, *pyg* is Welsh for pitch, and pitch was taken up this route to the copper mines (now in ruins) on the shores of Llyn Llydaw and Glaslyn. The track passes above Llyn Llydaw

TOP SIGHTS

❶ *Centre for Alternative Technology, Machynlleth: eco-centre set in a former quarry, with interactive displays, a cliff railway and activities.*

❷ *Conwy Castle: one of Edward I's masterpieces, overlooking the River Conwy.*

❸ *Ffestiniog Railway: steam railway running between Blaenau Ffestiniog and Porthmadog.*

❹ *Harlech Castle: stands in a wonderful position overlooking Cardigan Bay.*

❺ *Llechwedd Slate Caverns, Blaenau Ffestiniog: underground tours and a Victorian village.*

❻ *National Slate Museum, Padarn Country Park, Llanberis: workshops and machinery recalling the slate industry.*

❼ *Snowdon Mountain Railway: steam railway running from Llanberis to the summit.*

❽ *Swallow Falls, near Betws-y-Coed: classic beauty spot of waterfalls and woodland.*

ABOVE: Conwy Castle, on the northern edge of the park

TOP, LEFT TO RIGHT: Llanberis Pass; Harlech Castle, on its 200ft (60m) coastal crag

ABOVE: The Snowdon Mountain Railway

GREAT LITTLE TRAINS OF WALES

Although 90 per cent of visitors still arrive by car, Snowdonia is actually served by a good railway network. Betws-y-Coed can be reached by the Conwy Valley connection to the main London–Holyhead line, and Tywyn, Barmouth and Porthmadog are all on the Cambrian Coast line. However, the region is perhaps best known for its narrow-gauge railways, most of which were originally built to transport stone, slate and minerals from the mountains to ports on the coast.

The most famous is probably the Ffestiniog Railway, connecting Blaenau Ffestiniog with Porthmadog on the coast. Lesser known are the Llanberis Lake Railway, the Bala Lake Railway and the Tal-y-llyn Railway, which runs in the shadow of Cadair Idris in the south. The highest of them all, of course, is the rack-and-pinion Snowdon Mountain Railway, which has been conveying passengers the 4.5 miles (7km) to the 3,560ft (1,085m) summit for well over a century.

under the crags of Crib Goch to join the famous (and now reconstructed) interminable zigzags above Glaslyn to Carnedd Ugain and the ridge to the summit.

The Miners' Track is named for the men who worked the Llydaw and Glaslyn copper mines, and who probably walked up this route from Capel Curig to work every day. It is the most popular and most heavily engineered of all the paths up to the summit of Snowdon, and there is usually a crocodile of walkers along its 3.5-mile (5.6km) length. It takes a lower course than the Pyg Track, and crosses Llyn Llydaw by a causeway originally built to take the loads of ore extracted from the mines above.

There is one other popular ascent route from Pen-y-Pass: the Crib Goch route, which traverses the formidable rocky arête of Crib Goch ('the red comb or crest') – but it is not recommended for inexperienced walkers. The route up to the Snowdon summit via Crib Goch and the descent via the serrated summit of Lliwedd across from Glaslyn is known as the Snowdon Horseshoe. This is a 7.5-mile (12km) test for all proficient hill walkers and scramblers, and again should not be undertaken by inexperienced walkers.

The 4-mile (6.4km) Llanberis Path direct from the village is the least demanding but longest route to the summit, and parallels the mountain railway for much of its length. The best ascent from the south is the Watkin Path, which leads up from Nant Gwynant and passes the isolated Gladstone Rock. From here, at the grand age of 84, William Gladstone (1809–98) addressed the Welsh nation on freedom for small states. No doubt he would be delighted at the creation of the Welsh Assembly in 1997.

Western ascent routes include the popular Snowdon Ranger Path, which goes up from the Snowdon Ranger Youth Hostel by the peaceful shores of Llyn Cwellyn. This may have been the earliest regular ascent route to the summit. It was certainly used by Thomas Pennant (1726–98), the Welsh naturalist who left us a vivid description of dawn on the summit after his overnight ascent in *A Tour in Wales*, published in 1783. The other western route to the summit is the Rhyd-Ddu Path via Llechog from the Beddgelert to Caernarfon road.

So popular are the paths up and around Snowdon that constant repair work is necessary. The Snowdonia Upland Footpath Scheme was a £1.5 million European-funded partnership between the National Park Authority, the Countryside Council for Wales and the National Trust. The scheme also created many local jobs, improved the area's skills base and benefited the landscape, which was in grave danger of being loved to death.

Just across the Llanberis Pass, the rock-strewn landscape of the Glyderau is perhaps the wildest, most primeval landscape in Wales. The summits are covered with a chaotic jumble of huge blocks of rock, some piled on top of one another, others – like the Cantilever Stone on Glyder Fach – balanced precariously out from the main mass.

When Charles Kingsley, author of *The Water Babies*, described the astonishing scene in 1857 as an 'enormous desolation, the dead bones of the eldest born of time', he might well have had the powerful splintered mass of the Castle of the Winds on Glyder Fach in mind.

LEFT: *The Castle of the Winds and Glyder Fawr (in the background on the right) from Glyder Fach*

TOP: *The Ffestiniog Railway, which runs 14 miles (22km) between Porthmadog and Blaenau Ffestiniog*

The agent behind this lunar landscape was the one that executed the final shaping of the Snowdonia landscape we admire today. The last, grinding glaciers of the last Ice Age disappeared only about 10,000 years ago, and they left behind the U-shaped valleys, *cwmoedd*, glacial lakes, moraines and numerous erratic boulders that litter so many of Snowdonia's slopes. Frost shattering was the main cause behind the Glyderau's fantastic moonscape, and if you are ever up there in frosty, winter conditions, you can well believe it.

TOP: Swallow Falls near Betws-y-Coed

MAN'S INFLUENCE

But what of the human influence on Snowdonia? Traces of man's presence date back over 6,000 years to neolithic settlers, and evidence of these early farmers and the subsequent Bronze Age still exists in the foundations of their hut circles and burial mounds. Extensive trading activity was practised by these so-called 'primitive' people who made stone axes on Penmaenmawr Mountain, to the northeast of the national park, which were then transported all over the country.

It was once thought that the Romans barely ventured into the Celtic stronghold of the mountain fastnesses of Snowdonia, but more recent research has discovered a string of Roman forts along the north coast between Conwy and Caernarfon, with Segontium at Caernarfon being their regional headquarters. Walkers can still follow parts of their major north–south artery, the road known as Sarn Helen, built to subdue the Celts.

The shadowy figure of King Arthur may have been a Romano-British guerilla leader who was based in these mountains to lead the resistance during the Dark Ages against the invading Saxons, and who still waits in his cave on Lliwedd to come to the nation's rescue. But the truth is that we will probably never know for sure.

It was the Normans, and in particular the Plantagenet King Edward I, who really imposed their might on the rebellious tribes of Snowdonia and the rest of Wales. Edward's string of imposing castles, built in a very short time by craftsmen drawn from all over Britain, still lord it over the landscape – as he had intended they would. The great castles of Caernarfon, Conwy, Harlech, Criccieth and Castell y Bere (at Abergynolwyn) are major visitor attractions today, but when they were built they presented an unwelcome deterrent to any local inhabitants planning an uprising. They now form part of the Castles and Walls of King Edward World Heritage Site.

The advent of tourism coincided with Thomas Telford's Holyhead road to the Irish ferries – now known as the A5 – and the coming of the railways, many of which were originally built to carry slate to the burgeoning industrial cities of the Industrial Revolution (see panel, page 201).

Quarries extracting the easily accessible Ordovician slates of Snowdonia sliced great holes out of the landscape, notably around Llanberis and Blaenau Ffestiniog (which were excluded from the national park because of their unsightly slate quarries) and Corris. Now, the slate-quarrying industry (see panel, page 194) is celebrated in visitor attractions that explain how the rocks were quarried, often under atrocious conditions, and it remains an important part of Snowdonia's cultural heritage.

MODERN SNOWDONIA

Today, tourism is one of the main industries of Snowdonia, and a recent survey estimated that in the national park it supported around 4,000 jobs and contributed £66 million to the Gross Domestic Product of Wales.

As a mountaineering playground, the peaks of the area are second to none south of Skye, while Llyn Tegid near Bala, Wales's largest natural lake, offers excellent watersports and coarse fishing. Then there is cycling, whitewater rafting and glorious walks galore for all levels of fitness. Add to the mix Edward's castles, the Great Little Trains, gardens, woollen mills, family attractions and more, and it is easy to see why so many people come here.

North Wales and Snowdonia are still strongholds of Welsh nationalism and the Welsh language. In the park, two-thirds of the inhabitants claim Welsh as their first language. The Welsh word *Hiraeth* perhaps best sums up the fierce, proud Welshness of Snowdonia; it is difficult to translate precisely into English but it somehow evokes the magic and spirit of these magnificent, challenging and beguiling hills.

ABOVE, LEFT TO RIGHT: Beddgelert; Llyn Tegid (Bala lake); the Roman Steps in the Rhinogs – in fact a medieval packhorse route

LOCH LOMOND & THE TROSSACHS

When the distinguished Scottish mountaineer and writer W. H. 'Bill' Murray (1913–1996) wrote his seminal survey of Scottish landscapes, *Highland Landscapes*, in 1962, he confessed he thought it was little short of miraculous that the bonnie banks of Loch Lomond had remained free from unsightly tourism developments for so long.

THE BONNIE, BONNIE BANKS

Seventy per cent of Scotland's population now live within an hour of the national park, and visitor numbers are up to more than four million per annum. Hence Loch Lomond and the Trossachs National Park faces visitor pressures not experienced by other parks – with the possible exception of the Peak District, Lake District and South Downs – despite being the fourth largest in the family, covering 720 square miles (1,864sq km) of the area surrounding Loch Lomond and the Trossachs to the east. There is, of course, a high passing trade, estimated at three million a year, of visitors heading north up the A82 – the main north–south link to the Highlands and Islands of the northwest running along the western banks of Loch Lomond.

The National Park Authority admits the park suffers from the 'honeypot' syndrome. Some parts of it get many more visitors than others; these 'hot spots' are around the southern shores of Loch Lomond and Loch Katrine in the Trossachs, at places like Balloch, Luss and Callander. The visitor survey made in 2002 showed that more than 61 per cent are day visitors from the surrounding towns and cities of Scotland's central belt, and 63 per cent of all visitors came from within Scotland.

However, visitors have been thronging to Loch Lomond and the Trossachs since well before it became the long-awaited first national park in Scotland in 2002. It was probably the popular historical romances written by Sir Walter Scott (1771–1832) that really put the area on the tourist map. His poem *Lady of the Lake* (published in 1810) and his novel *Rob Roy* (published in 1817, see panel, page 210) first brought the attractions of Loch Lomond and the Trossachs to the attention of a wider public in the early years of the 19th century.

Good public transport links to places like Glasgow and Dumbarton and other towns in the central belt of Scotland meant that Loch Lomond was accessible to a large population.

LEFT: Loch Arklet: beyond is Ben Vane, part of the Arrochar Alps

Apart from the West Highland line, there were three other railway routes linking towns and villages, and at one time there was even a tramway between Balloch and Glasgow.

What attracts visitors is the subtle mixture of the beauty of loch and mountain and the vital, softening aspect of the extensive areas of semi-natural deciduous woodland, much of which was regularly coppiced to supply the needs of the newly emerging industrial city of Glasgow. But the popularity of the traditional song *Loch Lomond* (see panel, opposite) indicates that the area has held a special place in the affections of local people for many years prior to the writings of Scott and the arrival of the railway.

As long ago as 1771, Tobias Smollett (1721–71) wrote in *Humphry Clinker* that: 'Everything here is romantic beyond imagination. This country is justly styled the Arcadia of Scotland.'

MARVELS OF LOCH LOMOND

Loch Lomond was long famed for its three marvels, expressed in the doggerel verse:

> *Waves without Wind*
> *Fish without Fins*
> *And a Floating Island*

Strangely enough, all have perfectly plausible, natural explanations. The 'waves without wind' are undoubtedly 'seiches', the name given to the fluctuation of an enclosed body of water caused by rapid changes in barometric pressure. They can regularly be seen when a strong wind suddenly drops, allowing the 'piled-up' water on the windward side of the loch to move back in the opposite direction, thus apparently causing waves without wind. This phenomenon is usually quite short in duration, but one exceptional seiche recorded on Loch Lomond lasted for well over 12 hours.

The 'fish without fins' are probably lampreys – finless, eel-like fish once traditionally regarded in the Highlands as a fish of bad omen. There is a population of sea lampreys found in Loch Lomond all year round, which is odd because most of the other British populations breed in freshwater and migrate to the sea as adults. Lampreys are sometimes known as 'nine-eyed eels' because of the eye-like circular gill openings on both sides of the head, and they feed by locking themselves onto their prey with the disc-like structure that surrounds their mouth. Lampreys are among the 15 native species of fish found in the loch, which also include the rare Ice Age survivor the powan, a freshwater whitefish found only here and in Loch Eck, in Argyll and Bute. It is a protected species.

TOP: Trees in the Garadhban Forest at the foot of Conic Hill

BY YON BONNIE BANKS

The traditional Scottish folk song Loch Lomond may appear to be no more than a wistful love song, but in fact it has a more tragic origin.

One of Bonnie Prince Charlie's ill-fated Jacobite followers is said to have composed it as he languished under lock and key on the eve of his execution in Carlisle Castle. The famous opening lines, 'O, ye'll tak the high road and I'll tak the low road, And I'll be in Scotland afore ye', apparently refer to the last meeting of the soldier and his sweetheart. The girl had come from Loch Lomondside to bid a last farewell to her beloved and would return by the 'high road', while the condemned man would be taking the 'low road' to his grave the next day.

Another version of the story suggests that the spirit of the writer would return quicker to his native land after his death than his friend, who would be travelling by the ordinary 'high road'.

TOP: I Vow is the unusual name of this isle on Loch Lomond

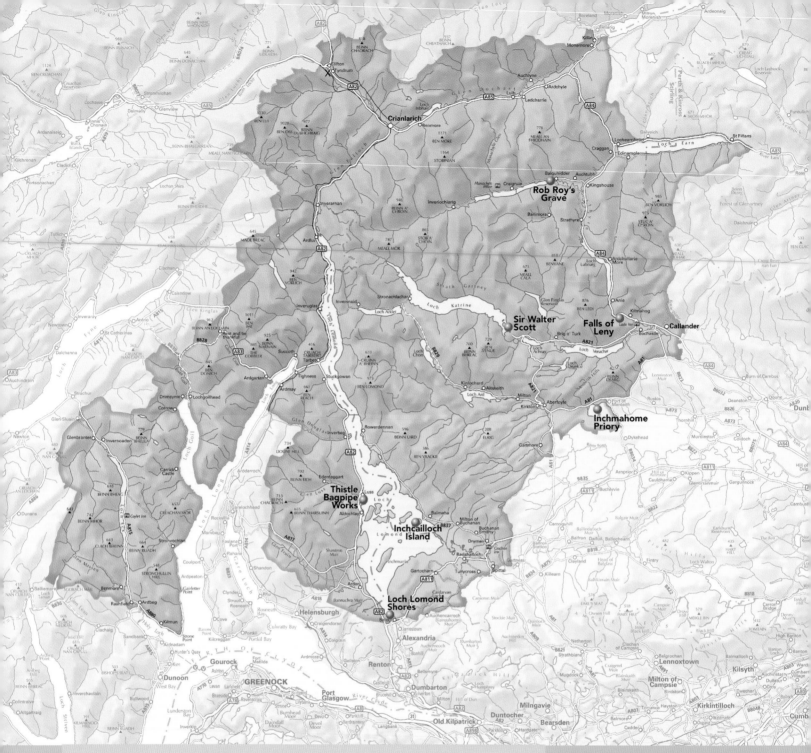

TOP SIGHTS

1 *Falls of Leny, near Kilmahog: a beauty spot in the Pass of Leny.*

2 *Inchcailloch Island, Loch Lomond: part of the Loch Lomond National Nature Reserve.*

3 *Inchmahome Priory (HS), reached by ferry from Port of Menteith: a ruined Augustinian priory on an island in the Lake of Menteith.*

4 *Loch Lomond Shores, Balloch: the principal gateway to the national park.*

5 *Rob Roy's Grave, in the kirkyard at Balquhidder: pay homage to the Jacobite and cattle thief Rob Roy MacGregor (1671–1734).*

6 *Sir Walter Scott: steamer on Loch Katrine.*

7 *Thistle Bagpipe Works, Luss: kilt and bagpipe makers, plus items to buy.*

The 'floating island' can also be explained. When a mat of shoreland vegetation and moss breaks loose after a flood or a sudden storm, it can appear like a green island floating across the surface of the loch. However, these 'islands' rarely seem to last for very long – unlike the numerous crannogs, or ancient loch dwellings, which have been discovered around the loch shores and were built as defensive homesteads mainly during the Iron Age (about 400BC).

Loch Lomond stands at the point where two worlds collided about 400 million years ago, and as a result it lies on the border between the mountainous Highlands and the gently undulating Lowlands of Scotland. In fact, the Highland Boundary Fault, one of the greatest known fractures in the Earth's crust, cuts right across the loch, between Ben Bowie to the southwest and Conic Hill to the northeast.

It can be seen by the naked eye if you stand on the craggy summit of Conic Hill on the West Highland Way and look southwest, across the obvious line created by the islands of Inchcailloch, Crenich and Inchmurrin, to the distant Ben Bowie and the steep slopes of Killoeter. The fault continues on northeast towards the Trossachs via the steep northwestern escarpment of the Menteith Hills and on towards Callander.

Loch Lomond also exhibits this topographical dichotomy by having two very different and distinct parts. The upper, northern end occupies a deep and narrow defile between the rugged hills of Arrochar, sometimes known as 'the Arrochar Alps', and Breadalbane to the west, and the reigning peak of Ben Lomond (3,194ft/974m) and its outliers to the east. The northern end of the loch has more of the feel of a Highland glen, with steep walls of rock rearing straight up from the water, while the broader,

LEFT: Inchmahome Priory, now in the care of Historic Scotland
TOP: Canoeing on Loch Lubhair, with Meall Glas as a backdrop

ABOVE, LEFT TO RIGHT: Walkers on the West Highland Way with the Crianlarich Hills beyond; Highland cow; Ben Lomond

less mountainous southern end is studded with 39 islands or 'inches' (not counting the floating ones!), and gives more of an impression of an Irish lowland lough.

One of the most interesting of Loch Lomond's islands is the wooded island of Inchcailloch, which is usually reached from Balmaha. The name means 'the island of the old women' and, as it lies precisely on the Highland Boundary Fault, it is part of the Loch Lomond National Nature Reserve, with a nature trail and camping and barbecue sites. There is an ancient church settlement and the remains of a convent dedicated to St Kentigerna, and the evocative graveyard is the burial place for many MacGregors and MacFarlanes. Wildlife on Inchcailloch includes a large population of garden warblers, unmatched elsewhere in northern Britain.

The reigning peaks of Ben Lui at 3,708ft (1,130m) and Ben Ime at 3,318ft (1,011m) dominate Breadalbane and the Arrochar Alps, but perhaps the most charismatic mountain on the western side of the loch is Ben Arthur. Familiarly known in the climbing world as the Cobbler, this craggy, triple-summit peak is not even a Munro (a summit of more than 3,000ft/914m) because it rises to only 2,900ft (883m). Nevertheless, it is a true mountain summit that can only be fully traversed by the use of hands, so many people prefer to stop at the Central Peak between the precipitous South and overhanging North Peaks, which are known as the Cobbler's Wife and the Cobbler's Last respectively.

The mountain scene that makes up the western frame of the loch has been materially altered by the construction of the Loch Sloy dam and its accompanying reservoir, between Ben Vorlich and

ABOVE, LEFT TO RIGHT: Loch Arklet; Loch Earn

RIGHT: Ben Arthur, better known as the Cobbler

Ben Vane. The water conduit pipes and power lines feed down to the monolithic Inveruglas hydroelectric plant on the A82. On the opposite side of the loch and beneath the northern slopes of Ben Lomond, Loch Arklet has been similarly artificially enlarged by a dam and provides fresh Highland water to Glasgow and other towns in the Central Belt.

The narrow, 1.5-mile (2.4km) neck of land between Tarbet and Arrochar village, linking Loch Lomond and the linear sea inlet of Loch Long, was apparently used by the raiding Viking forces of King Haakon of Norway in 1263, who dragged their longships on wooden rollers across country to reach the loch. The only natural outlet of Loch Lomond is the River Leven, which flows into the mighty Clyde estuary.

THE TROSSACHS

In *Highland Landscapes*, Bill Murray considered that the panorama from the Trossachs hills – especially from the comparatively lowly Ben Venue (2,386ft/727m) and Ben An (1,520ft/463m) – was excellent and out of all proportion to their height. He thought the best times to visit the Trossachs were in spring, 'when the birch and oak come alive in new green and yellow, when hard on the primroses' heels bluebells spread a haze through the woodland', and in the autumn 'when the dying bracken makes on each hill a blaze like a Viking's pyre'.

It is the wild pass between Ben Venue and Ben An that gives access to the area whose name is said to mean 'the rough or bristly country'. This wild and woolly country was for long the

haunt of cattle rustlers and thieves, like Rob Roy MacGregor (see panel, page 210). The name of the pass at the eastern end of Loch Katrine and below the slopes of Ben Venue gives a clue to its turbulent past. Bealach nam Bo literally means 'the pass of the cattle', and this was where the bandit MacGregors and others drove their stolen booty into the secret heart of the mountains.

The name Trossachs is now more generally applied to the triangle of mountains and woodland between Loch Katrine, Aberfoyle and Callander, all of which now falls within the national park. Loch Katrine looks entirely natural in its mountain setting, but its water level is artificially controlled, as it is a reservoir for Glasgow Corporation. A highlight for many visitors is a trip up the loch on the steamer *Sir Walter Scott*, which was built as long ago as 1900 and now is in its second century of service.

Purists, however, prefer the intimacy of the smaller, tree-lined Loch Achray or 'the crooked loch', Loch Lubnaig, which lies over the Pass of Leny with its spectacular Falls of Leny, to the northeast. One of the most intriguing names in the Trossachs is the Wood of Lamentation, which lies alongside the A821 road on the northern side of Loch Venachar. In days gone by, children were warned to stay away from the waterside in case the *each uishge*, a mystical water horse similar to Loch Ness's fabled monster, should lure them into the water to their deaths.

The fact is that the loch has shallow shelves of rock around its edges, tempting people, particularly children, to wade into the comparatively warm water. But the bottom then drops quickly

LEFT: Ben Venue and the Achray Hotel reflected in Loch Achray

TOP, LEFT TO RIGHT: Loch Ard, near Aberfoyle; view to Ben An

and steeply into the icy depths of the loch, and tragically many people have drowned, including children, over the years. So the name of the wood echoes the lamentations of the parents of the victims of the legendary *each uishge*, or the spirit of the loch.

Loch Venachar, like Loch Katrine and several of the other lochs in the Trossachs, is now a reservoir, so its character is much changed since Walter Scott used it as the setting for the gathering place of the clans in *The Lady of the Lake*. The name is ancient and was first recorded as *Bheann-chair* in Gaelic.

This is usually translated as 'the pointed loch', but its literal meaning of 'horns cast' might indicate that this was where the abundant herds of red deer that roamed the area cast their antlers every year.

The slopes of Ben Ledi, simply known as 'The Ben' in these parts, sweep up from the northern shores of Loch Venachar, and the shapely mountain dominates the westward views from Callander. This dominance has given the mountain an almost spiritual presence, and one explanation of its Gaelic name

ABOVE: *Red deer stags, Britain's largest land mammal*

Ben le Dia is 'the mountain of God' or 'of light'. Townsfolk and visitors frequently climb it, and in days gone by it was known as a Beltane hill, or *La Buidhe Bealltuinn*, which translates as 'the yellow day of the fires of Bel'.

On the Celtic New Year, the first of May, young people of the locality would meet on the 2,875ft (876m) summit to commemorate the ancient rite of the lighting of the Beltane fires in honour of the Celtic sun god. Down below, all fires were extinguished before midnight and then relit from the purifying flames from the top of the mountain. Sometimes cattle were driven between the fires in the belief that this would protect them from disease during the coming year.

The main town serving the Trossachs is Callander, at the easternmost extremity of the national park. Callander is both a frontier and a gateway to the Highlands. The Crown Estate Commissioners, who took over the Clan Drummond lands after the 1745 Jacobite Rebellion, laid out the town's broad main streets and square.

But these were not the first settlements in the area: at Dunmore, above the A821, there is an Iron Age fort, and the remains of a Roman marching camp have been identified just outside the town at Bochastle. Outside the old red sandstone church dedicated to the Celtic St Kessog in Ancaster Square you will often see Highland dancing being performed to music provided by a pipe band.

Just to the south of the Trossachs, on the edge of the park, lies the peaceful, lowland Lake of Menteith, sometimes erroneously known as Scotland's only lake (in fact, several lochs are called lakes). Its most striking feature is the romantic ruins of the priory on the island of Inchmahome, reached by a short ferry trip from Port of Menteith. Walter Comyn, Earl of Menteith, brought the monks to Inchmahome in 1238, and it was known to Robert the Bruce and Mary, Queen of Scots, who was sent there for her safety when she was a child after Henry VIII had made it known that he wanted her to marry his son, Edward.

The celebrated poet Gerard Manley Hopkins (1844–89) was a visitor to Inversnaid on the wild eastern bank of Loch Lomond in 1881. He arrived by steamer on a day trip and was so impressed by the wildness of the situation that he wrote one of his most famous poems, *Inversnaid*, about it. It is a fitting *envoi* to our journey around Loch Lomond and the Trossachs National Park:

> *What would the world be, once bereft
> Of wet and wilderness? Let them be left,
> O let them be left, wilderness and wet,
> Long live the weeds and the wilderness yet.*

TOP, LEFT TO RIGHT: The Falls of Dochart in Killin; Loch Achray, with Ben Venue in the background

ABOVE: The beach at Luss below Ben Lomond
RIGHT: The Sir Walter Scott steamer on Loch Katrine

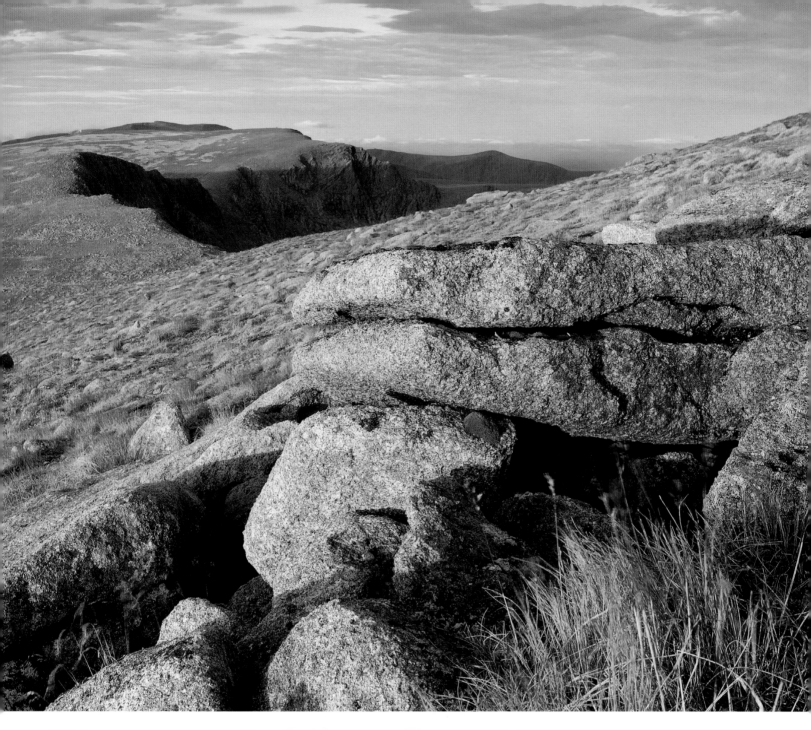

ABOVE, LEFT TO RIGHT: The Cairngorm funicular railway; Scottish crossbill; mountain biker along Gleann ant-Slugain

THE BIG GREY MAN OF BEN MACDUI

Ben Macdui is not only the highest mountain in the Cairngorms and the second highest in Britain, it can also lay claim to being haunted.

It is the alleged home of the so-called Big Grey Man, or *An Fear Liath Mor*, a spectral being who is often heard or sensed, but seldom seen. The first man to record the phenomenon was Dr Norman Collie, a distinguished climber and the first Professor of Organic Chemistry at the University of London, in 1891. He told his story in 1925 at the AGM of the Cairngorm Club,

Scotland's oldest mountaineering club, of which he was an honorary president.

Collie related that he had been returning from the summit on a misty day when he heard someone – or something – walking after him. 'Seized with terror', he took to his heels.

Other climbers have since reported not only hearing but seeing the Big Grey Man on the mountain, but it should perhaps be noted that Dr Collie had something of a reputation as a prankster.

TOP: *Ben Macdui, from Glen Lui near Braemar*
ABOVE: *Looking west from Ben Macdui*

in the shadow of Ben Macdui, at 4,296ft (1,309m) the highest mountain in the range and the second-highest mountain in Britain (see panel, opposite) after Ben Nevis. Five of Scotland's nine 4,000ft (1,219m) summits dominate the range, plus a further nine mountains that are higher than 3,500ft (1,066m) and four more that exceed 3,000ft (914m). The 'Big Five' are Ben Macdui, Braeriach, Cairn Gorm, Cairn Toul and Sgor an Lochain Uaine.

SUMMITS AND SANDY BEACHES

A vast, horseshoe-shaped plateau sweeps round from Ben Macdui to Cairn Gorm (4,081ft/1,244m), the principal summit in view from Aviemore and the Spey valley, and the mountain (meaning 'blue hill') that has given its name to the whole range. Ben Macdui's encircling ridges shelter two of Britain's most spectacular and remote mountain lakes. Loch Etchachan, described earlier, is the highest lake of any size in Britain, while Loch Avon lies like a beautiful jewel in the glacial trough between Ben Macdui, Beinn Mheadhoin and Cairn Gorm. Ringed by lovely beaches of fine white and golden sands, Loch

Avon (or A'an) is 1.5 miles (2.4km) long and up to 1,000ft (304m) wide. It is watched over by the famous Shelter Stone, a massive, house-sized fallen boulder. The Sticil, or Shelter Stone Crag, at the head of the loch has been used by generations of hillwalkers as a refuge from the biting Cairngorm wind, rain and snow.

The other 4,000ft (1,219m) tops of the Cairngorms lie to the west of the Lairig Ghru. Braeriach, the third-highest mountain in Britain at 4,252ft (1,296m), is the northernmost, while a glorious ridge sweeps south to the beautiful cones of Sgor an Lochain Uaine, also known as the Angel's Peak (4,127ft/1,257m), and Cairn Toul (4,236ft/1,291m). Cairn Toul's shapely southern outlier, the wickedly named Devil's Point at 3,294ft (1,004m), has the simple shelter of the Corrour bothy (see panel, page 229) at its foot. The literal meaning of the mountain's Gaelic name, *Bod an Deamhain*, is 'the Devil's penis'.

The Braeriach plateau ends abruptly in the west by the deep, glacial chasm of Glen Einich, containing beautiful Loch Einich

ABOVE: Climbing the summit tor on Ben Avon

TOP SIGHTS

❶ Balmoral Castle, between Ballater and Braemar: the Scottish home of the royal family since Queen Victoria bought it in 1848.

❷ Blair Castle, Blair Atholl: home of the Duke of Atholl.

❸ Braemar Highland Heritage Centre, Braemar: exhibition on the history of Braemar.

❹ Cairngorm Reindeer Centre, Glenmore, Aviemore: where you can go with a herder and get up close to reindeer.

❺ Glenlivet Distillery, Glenlivet, Ballindalloch: tour the distillery and have a dram.

❻ Glenmore Visitor Centre and Forest Park, Glenmore: lots of watersports, forest trails and a visitor centre.

❼ Highland Wildlife Park, Kincraig: see wolves, wildcats, beavers and otters.

❽ Loch Garten Osprey Centre, by Boat of Garten: overlooks nesting ospreys (see panel, page 230).

❾ Rothiemurchus Visitor Centre, Inverdruie, Aviemore: guided walks and safari tours.

❿ Royal Lochnagar Distillery and Visitor Centre, Crathie, Ballater: another chance to tour a distillery and enjoy a single malt.

⓫ Strathspey Railway, Aviemore Station: steam trains run between Aviemore, Boat of Garten, Broomhill and Grantown on Spey.

WELCOME BACK, RUDOLF

According to the ancient Orkneyinga saga, red deer and reindeer were hunted together by the Earls of Orkney in Caithness about eight centuries ago. We also know, from fossil records, that reindeer were common much further south after the last Ice Age.

When the Swedish reindeer breeder Mikel Utsi visited the Rothiemurchus Forest in the late 1940s, he was immediately struck by the similarity of the Cairngorms landscape to the reindeer pastures of Lapland. So, in 1952, he resolved to introduce some Swedish mountain reindeer to Scotland as an experiment on 300 acres (120ha) near Aviemore, and the herd has since grown to its present size of between 130 and 150 animals.

Reindeer, which calve in May and June, require very little management. They are bred for their meat and hide, and for their antlers, which are carved into craft items. Visitors can see reindeer in their natural environment by joining a trip from the Cairngorm Reindeer Centre at Glenmore, near Aviemore, and other 'former residents' like wolves and bison can be seen at the Highland Wildlife Park at Kincraig.

at its head. To the south of Glen Einich is a remote plateau known as the Moine Mhor (or 'great moss'). The third group of Cairngorm summits lies to the east of the Derry Burn and is dominated by tor-topped Beinn a'Bhuird at 3,927ft (1,197m) and Ben Avon at 3,842ft (1,171m). The Cairngorms truly are a Munroist's paradise (see panel, page 227).

North and east of the main mountain mass, the braes lead gently down to the River Spey and the whisky capital of Glenlivet. The remains of the once-mighty Caledonian Forest soften the scene, perpetuated in the ancient pine forests of Glen Feshie, the Glenmore Forest Park, Rothiemurchus, and the Abernethy Forest, which surrounds the osprey-haunted Loch Garten.

To the south, across the National Trust for Scotland's Mar Lodge estate, near Braemar and the mighty eastward-flowing River Dee, lies the lofty White Mounth or Lochnagar plateau. It reaches its highest point at Lochnagar itself, a forbidding 3,789ft (1,155m)

north-facing amphitheatre of crags and deep gullies much beloved of ice climbers in winter. The range gradually relents as it spreads eastwards down the broad reaches of Glen Muick towards the town of Ballater. The Glenshee skiing area lies to the west of the White Mounth, where the A93 road slices through the range via the Devil's Elbow.

RARE FINDS

The harsh, tundra-like climate and the vegetation of the Cairngorms mean that many British rarities grow here, some of which are only found elsewhere beyond the Arctic Circle or in the Alps. Apparently, a quarter of the 400 rare and endangered British species are found within the national park. Examples of these include the three-pointed rush, dwarf willow and dwarf cudweed. Crowberry and blaeberry occupy the more sheltered spots, while heather is more common in the surrounding foothills, often colonising the surface of glacial moraines. The most characteristic bird of the high Cairngorm tops is the

ABOVE, LEFT TO RIGHT: Red squirrel; Braeriach and Loch Einich from Sgor Gaoith; Balmoral Castle and Lochnagar

ptarmigan, which is seldom seen below around 2,000ft (600m). This is the only British bird to change its plumage to a creamy white as camouflage against the expected, but no longer certain, winter snowfall. Visitors to the igloo-shaped Ptarmigan restaurant on Cairn Gorm summit may see excitable little flocks of black-and-white snow buntings flitting around the summit boulders.

Less likely to be spotted, but nonetheless present, is the magnificent golden eagle. This is one of the most exciting birds in Britain, and it still has a stronghold in the Cairngorms. There has been a steady increase in numbers of this most powerful and charismatic of raptors, but there are still worrying cases of illegal persecution every year.

Another reminder of Ice Age Britain is the presence of Britain's only herd of wild reindeer, which roam the area of the Glenmore Forest Park, south of Loch Morlich. A Swedish reindeer herder, Mikel Utsi, introduced these large animals in 1952, and the Cairngorm herd has grown to its present size of between 130 and 150 animals (see panel, page 225). Lower down, in the more sheltered valleys of the Spey and Dee, the last remains of Scotland's primeval forest are found. However, the ancient Scots pines found, for example, on the NTS's Mar Lodge estate east of Braemar are nothing like the slim, spindly Scots pines found further south. These trees have massive girths supporting a full rounded head of branches. Those that have reached 200 to 300 years old or more are known to foresters as 'granny pines'.

These ancient pine forests are home to some fascinating wildlife, not least the red squirrel and Britain's largest game bird, the turkey-sized, black-feathered capercaillie. Once you have heard the weird call of the male capercaillie, you will never forget it. It starts with a resonant rattle and continues with a popping noise, like drawing a cork, followed by the sound of pouring liquid. Higher up among the pine needles, the metallic-sounding 'chip, chip' of the Scottish crossbill may also be heard. These colourful (the males are crimson and the females green-grey) seed-eaters, along with the more widespread common crossbill,

LEFT: Golden eagle
TOP: The summit cairn on Cairn Gorm mountain

ABOVE, LEFT TO RIGHT: Glen Muick; Rothiemurchus Forest; a furry-footed ptarmigan in winter plumage

are the only birds in Britain that have the tips of their beaks crossed, which enables them to winkle out the pine seeds from their cones. Scottish crossbills, members of the finch family, are a protected species in Scotland. Other birds that breed in the pine forests include the crested tit, wood sandpiper, golden eagle and redwing, with common goldeneye on the lochs. Loch Garten, sheltered in the pines of the Abernethy Forest on Speyside, was the scene of one of the most successful returns of a British breeding species for 50 years when osprey returned to breed here in the mid-1950s (see panel, page 230). Since then,

thousands of birders have enjoyed the sight of this majestic raptor flying above the water to locate a fish, which it then catches by plunge diving, at the RSPB's Loch Garten Osprey Centre. Also known as the seahawk or fish eagle, this special bird of prey overwinters in Africa and can be seen here between late March and September.

ROADS AND RAILWAYS

The cultural heritage of the Cairngorms can be traced back to the end of the last Ice Age, and the Blue Cairn of Balnagowan

TOP: Loch Morlich, with the Cairngorms under a blanket of cloud

MOUNTAIN BOTHIES

In places like the Cairngorms where 'the long walk in' to reach many mountains is the norm, there is always the danger of being benighted in the hills. That's when the mountain bothies, such as the one at Corrour, below the Devil's Point at the southern end of the Lairig Ghru, can literally be lifesavers.

The Mountain Bothies Association is a charity that looks after about 100 shelters in remote parts of the UK. Most bothies are stone buildings with a slate or corrugated iron roof, like that at Corrour. They range in size from the equivalent of a garden shed to two-storey cottages with six or seven rooms.

Bothies are reasonably wind- and water-tight, but you must remember to bring your own sleeping bag. They generally have a fireplace or a stove, but you will need to bring fuel, or, if wood has been left by a previous visitor, the tradition is that you gather enough to replace what you burn – and take your litter home.

THE RETURN OF THE OSPREY

The sight of a magnificent black-and-white osprey swooping low over Loch Garten, in the north of the Cairngorms, to snatch a fish from the water and return to its tree-top nest is one of the most exciting wildlife encounters you'll have. And the return of this rare raptor to these Scottish hills is one of the great environmental success stories of recent years.

In 1959 the RSPB made the inspirational decision to allow public viewing of a pair of breeding ospreys –the only breeding pair in the country – at Loch Garten. This was a courageous decision because, at that time, gamekeepers and egg collectors were persecuting this handsome bird and, even after the RSPB allowed the public in, there were several instances of egg theft. But the decision proved to be a great public relations coup. Since then, over two million people have visited the RSPB Loch Garten Osprey Centre, near Boat of Garten, to enjoy the birds. Nno single dynasty of birds has done more to engender such a positive response to nature and it was appropriate that a stylised osprey was developed as a brand for the park.

near Aboyne and the Lagmore Clava Cairn near Ballindalloch provide evidence of how these early settlers buried their dead.

But it was the Celts and Picts who gave birth to the clan system, savagely dismantled after the ill-fated Jacobite rebellion of 1715. Evidence of these troubled times can still be seen in the impressive ruined barracks used by the Hanoverian soldiers at Ruthven, near Kingussie, and Corgarff, which still cast their malevolent influence over the now empty landscape.

The Highlands were eventually tamed by the system of military roads built by General George Wade (1673–1748), who constructed over 240 miles (386km) of roads and 40 bridges between 1724 and 1740. In 1754, about 700 men were still working on the section of road between Braemar and Corgarff, and parts of this road can be traced today. In Victorian times, the railway opened up the area to tourism, and one of the first visitors was Queen Victoria. She and Prince Albert bought Balmoral Castle, near Braemar, as their holiday home, and the royal family still summer here.

As well as that sense of wilderness that cannot be experienced elsewhere in Britain, the Cairngorms offer holidaymakers a huge choice of outdoor activities – walking, cycling, angling and watersports opportunities are all superb – while Aviemore, Grantown on Spey, Kingussie, Ballater and Braemar are all convenient starting points for expeditions into the Cairngorms and of interest in their own right.

ABOVE, LEFT TO RIGHT: A cock capercaillie and his harem of females in Abernethy Forest; the Old Royal Station at Ballater

RIGHT: The Ruthven Barracks at Kingussie, built in 1719 after the Jacobite rising of 1715, and captured and burnt by Bonnie Prince Charlie in 1746

JEWELS IN THE CROWN

The British national parks have been a success. Described as 'the jewels in the crown' of our countryside, they act as valuable 'greenprints' for other areas involved in countryside conservation.

Among the many achievements of the national park authorities have been the continued protection of the parks against the most harmful developments; the promotion and support of public transport as a means of getting to and around the parks; the pioneering of open access by agreement; the conversion of disused railway lines into walking and riding trails; and farm-conservation schemes that have retained traditional landscapes.

More recently, in the light of the continuing threat of climate change, the role of traditional farming as creator and regulator of these well-loved landscapes has been questioned. Professor Adrian Phillips, a former Director General of the Countryside Commission, said that the idea of continuing to keep the greater parts of Britain's national parks farmed full time in the traditional way was 'unrealistic'. Phillips thought that traditional farming would be wound down in marginal areas, while some landscapes would be left to go wild both to protect biodiversity and to absorb more water in features like peat bogs, which are vitally important carbon sinks. This would help to reduce both the country's carbon emissions and the threat of flooding downstream. And farmers should be paid to follow this strategy.

So where do British national parks go from here? Now that Scotland is well and truly in the fold, is anywhere else still deserving of national park status? The President of the Campaign to Protect Rural England (CPRE), American-born author and journalist Bill Bryson, certainly seems to think so. In his inaugural address, he claimed that the whole of England was worthy of the status of a national park.

'Something I have often wondered is why we don't make the whole of England a national park,' he said. 'In what way, after all, are the Yorkshire Dales superior to the Durham Dales? Why is the New Forest worthy of exalted status but glorious Dorset unworthy? It is preposterous really to say that some parts are better or more important than others.'

Of course, Bryson's dream is very unlikely to happen. Only nine per cent of the area of England is currently designated as a national park, and the figure is similar in Scotland. Wales has the higher figure of 20 per cent because it is a much smaller country. Countryside lovers were delighted that, in April 2011, the South Downs was finally declared England's 10th and Britain's 15th national park. The Council for National Parks is still keeping a watching brief on another possible Welsh national park – the Cambrian Mountains, which was turned down after local opposition in 1974. Other possible candidates for national park status include the North Pennines, the so-called Jurassic Coast of Dorset (already a World Heritage Site), and the tempting prospect of a first national park for Northern Ireland – the granite mass of the Mountains of Mourne, south of Belfast.

In 2009, the people of the Isle of Harris in the Outer Hebrides voted more than two to one in favour of plans to make the entire island Scotland's third national park. But in January 2011, the Scottish Government announced that it would not consider a case for national park status for Harris in the current economic climate, and without the full support of the Western Isles Council (Comhairle nan Eilean Siar).

LEFT: The Mountains of Mourne, Northern Ireland

Recent boundary changes mean that some existing national parks are being extended. In October 2010, the Cairngorms National Park – already the UK's largest – got even bigger. The area known as Highland Perthshire and Glenshee was included, increasing the size of the park by one fifth, so that it now covers about six per cent of the total area of Scotland.

And as stated earlier, as this book went to press, consultations were still taking place over proposed extensions to both the Lake District and Yorkshire Dales national parks, which would effectively join the two north of Sedbergh. These changes, if ratified, would increase the area of the Yorkshire Dales National Park by nearly a quarter (24 per cent) and the Lake District by

three per cent. But recent government cuts have hit the parks hard. The Campaign for National Parks (CNP) reacted with dismay to the announcement at the end of 2010 that the English national park authorities will receive a 21.5 per cent cash reduction over the next four years, which, when taking inflation into account, amounted to a reduction of 28.5 per cent. Ruth Chambers, CNP's Head of Policy, said: 'These cuts may not sound so bad in the context of the government's plans to make overwhelming funding cuts across the board. But when inflation and the impact of secondary funding cuts are taken into account, the cuts will have a long-lasting and detrimental effect on the excellent work that these bodies do to look after national parks for the nation.'

NATIONAL PARKS FOR THE FUTURE?

❶ *Cambrian Mountains: the moorland and reservoir-dotted mass south of Snowdonia and north of the Brecon Beacons.*

❷ *Dorset Coast: the geologically important 'Jurassic Coast', a World Heritage Site, between Purbeck and Lyme Regis.*

❸ *Mountains of Mourne, Northern Ireland: granite mass of smoothly rounded peaks between Newcastle and Carlingford Lough.*

❹ *North Pennines: the northern Pennine moors between the Yorkshire Dales and Northumberland, already an Area of Outstanding Natural Beauty (AONB).*

TOP, LEFT TO RIGHT: Brandy Pad in the Mourne Mountains; the River Wye near Rhayader in the Cambrian Mountains

ABOVE: Durdle Door
RIGHT: The cliffs of Swyre Head, on Dorset's Jurassic Coast

USEFUL ADDRESSES

NATIONAL

Association of National Park Authorities
126 Bute Street, Cardiff Bay, Cardiff CF10 5LE
Tel: 029 2049 9966;
email: info@anpa.gov.uk;
www.nationalparks.gov.uk

Council for National Parks
6–7 Barnard Mews, London SW11 1QU
Tel: 020 7924 4077;
email: info@cnp.org.uk;
www.cnp.org.uk

ENGLAND

English National Park Authorities Association
1st Floor, 2–4 Great Eastern Street,
London EC2A 3NW
Tel: 020 7655 4812;
email: enquiries@enpaa.org.uk;
www.enpaa.org.uk

Natural England
1 East Parade, Sheffield, S1 2ET
Tel: 0845 600 3078;
email: enquiries@naturalengland.org.uk;
www.naturalengland.org.uk

Broads National Park Authority
18 Colegate, Norwich, Norfolk NR3 1BQ
Tel: 01603 610734;
email: broads@broads-authority.gov.uk;
www.broads-authority.gov.uk

Dartmoor National Park Authority
Parke, Haytor Road, Bovey Tracey,
Newton Abbot, Devon TQ13 9JQ
Tel: 01626 832093;
email: hq@dartmoor-npa.gov.uk;
www.dartmoor-npa.gov.uk

Exmoor National Park Authority
Exmoor House, Dulverton, Somerset TA22 9HL
Tel: 01398 323665;
email: info@exmoor-nationalpark.gov.uk;
www.exmoor-nationalpark.gov.uk

Lake District National Park Authority
Murley Moss, Oxenholme Road, Kendal,
Cumbria LA9 7RL
Tel: 01539 724555;
email: hq@lakedistrict.gov.uk;
www.lakedistrict.gov.uk

New Forest National Park Authority
South Efford House, Milford Road, Lymington,
Hampshire SO41 0JD
Tel: 01590 646600;
email: enquiries@newforestnpa.gov.uk;
www.newforestnpa.gov.uk

Northumberland National Park Authority
Eastburn, South Park, Hexham,
Northumberland NE46 1BS
Tel: 01434 605555;
email: enquiries@nnpa.org.uk;
www.northumberlandnationalpark.org.uk

North York Moors National Park Authority
The Old Vicarage, Bondgate, Helmsley,
North Yorkshire YO62 5BP
Tel: 01439 770657;
email: info@northyorkmoors-npa.gov.uk;
www.northyorkmoors.org.uk

Peak District National Park Authority
Aldern House, Baslow Road, Bakewell,
Derbyshire DE45 1AE
Tel: 01629 816200;
email: customer.service@peakdistrict.gov.uk;
www.peakdistrict.gov.uk

South Downs National Park Authority
Rosemary's Parlour, North Street, Midhurst,
West Sussex GU29 9SB
Tel: 0300 303 1053;
email: info@southdowns.gov.uk;
www.southdowns.gov.uk

Yorkshire Dales National Park Authority
Yoredale, Bainbridge, Leyburn,
North Yorkshire DL8 3EL
Tel: 0300 456 0030;
email: info@yorkshiredales.org.uk;
www.yorkshiredales.org.uk

WALES

Countryside Council for Wales
Maes y Ffynnon, Penrhosgarnedd, Bangor,
Gwynedd LL57 2DW
Tel: 0845 130 6229;
email: info@ccw.gov.uk;
www.ccw.gov.uk

Welsh Association of National Park Authorities
126 Bute Street, Cardiff Bay, Cardiff CF10 5LE
Tel: 029 2049 9966; email: nationalparkswales@
anpa.gov.uk; www.nationalparks.gov.uk

Brecon Beacons National Park Authority
Plas y Ffynnon, Cambrian Way, Brecon,
Powys LD3 7HP
Tel: 01874 624437;
email: enquiries@breconbeacons.org;
www.breconbeacons.org

Pembrokeshire Coast National Park Authority
Llanion Park, Pembroke Dock,
Pembrokeshire SA72 6DY
Tel: 0845 345 7275;
email: info@pembrokeshirecoast.org.uk;
www.pembrokeshirecoast.org.uk

Snowdonia National Park Authority
Penrhyndeudraeth, Gwynedd LL48 6LF
Tel: 01766 770274;
email: parc@snowdonia-npa.gov.uk;
www.snowdonia-npa.gov.uk

SCOTLAND

Council for National Parks, Scottish Office
An Tearmann, East Lewiston, Coiltyside,
Drumnadrochit, Inverness IV63 6UJ
Tel: 01456 450397;
email: info@scnp.org.uk;
www.scnp.org.uk

Scottish Natural Heritage
Great Glen House, Leachkin Road,
Inverness IV3 8NW
Tel: 01463 725000;
email: enquiries@snh.gov.uk;
www.snh.gov.uk

Cairngorms National Park Authority
14 The Square, Grantown on Spey,
Morayshire PH26 3HG
Tel: 01479 873535;
email: enquiries@cairngorms.co.uk;
www.cairngorms.co.uk

Loch Lomond & the Trossachs National Park Authority
Carrochan, Carrochan Road, Balloch
G83 8EG
Tel: 01389 722600;
email: info@lochlomond-trossachs.org;
www.lochlomond-trossachs.org

LEFT: Poppies are a familiar sight in the field margins of the South Downs

INDEX

ACKNOWLEDGEMENTS

The author and the Automobile Association wish to thank the National Park Authorities for their help with this book.

The Automobile Association wishes to thank the following photographers and organisations for their assistance in the preparation of this book.

Abbreviations for the picture credits are as follows – (t) top; (b) bottom; (l) left; (r) right; (c) centre; (AA) AA World Travel Library

4 AA/Adam Burton; 6tr Stuart Walker/Chris Bonington Picture Library; 7 AA/Stephen Lewis; 8 AA/Mike Kipling; 10-11 AA/A Mockford & N Bonetti; 12tl Peak District National Park Authority; 12tc Peak District National Park Authority; 12tr Peak District National Park Authority; 13 AA/A Mockford & N Bonetti; 14 AA/Chris Warren; 15tl AA/Wyn Voysey; 15tr AA/John Wood; 16 AA/Tom Mackie; 17 Michael Callan/FLPA; 18 John Hawkins/FLPA; 19bl AA/Dan Santillo; 19br AA/Tom Mackie; 20 AA/Guy Edwardes; 22-23 AA/Guy Edwardes; 24-25 AA/Guy Edwardes; 24bl AA/Nigel Hicks; 25bl AA/Nigel Hicks; 25br AA/Nigel Hicks; 26br AA/Nigel Hicks; 27 AA/Guy Edwardes; 28-29 AA/Guy Edwardes; 30 AA/Guy Edwardes; 31t AA/Guy Edwardes; 31bl AA/Guy Edwardes; 31bc AA/Guy Edwardes; 31br AA/Nigel Hicks; 32tl AA/Guy Edwardes; 32-33b AA/Guy Edwardes; 33t AA/Guy Edwardes; 34 AA/Steve Day; 36tl AA/Nigel Hicks; 36-37t Neville Stanikk/Cornish Picture Library; 36bl AA/Nigel Hicks; 36bc AA/Andrew Lawson; 36br AA/Nigel Hicks; 37bl AA/Nigel Hicks; 38tl AA/Nigel Hicks; 38tc AA/Nigel Hicks; 38tr AA/Nigel Hicks; 39tl AA/Nigel Hicks; 38-39b AA/Nigel Hicks; 40b AA/Nigel Hicks; 41t AA/Caroline Jones; 41bl AA/Nigel Hicks; 41bc AA/Nigel Hicks; 41br AA/Nigel Hicks; 42tl AA/Roger Moss; 42tr Gregory Goldston/Cornish Picture Library; 43 Powered by Light/Alan Spencer/Alamy; 44 Lisa Moore/Alamy; 45 AA/Roger Moss; 46-47b AA/Caroline Jones; 47tl Bert Hardy/Getty Images; 47r AA/Caroline Jones; 48 AA/Adam Burton; 50-51 AA/Adam Burton; 51br AA/Adam Burton; 52 AA/Wyn Voysey; 53tl AA/Adam Burton; 53bl AA/Adam Burton; 53bc Martin O'Neill/New Forest National Park; 53br AA/Adam Burton; 54bl AA/Wyn Voysey; 54-55 AA/Adam Burton; 56 AA/Adam Burton; 57t AA/Wyn Voysey; 57bl Martin O'Neill/New Forest National Park; 57bc AA/Adam Burton; 57br Martin O'Neill/New Forest National Park; 58-59 AA/Adam Burton; 60 AA/Adam Burton; 61 Martin O'Neill/New Forest National Park; 62 AA/John Miller; 64 Peter Lane/Alamy; 65bl AA/John Miller; 65br AA/John Miller; 67bl Laurie Noble; 67bc AA/John Miller; 67br AA/John Miller; 68tl Robin Chittenden/Alamy; 68tc Andy Rouse/NHPA/Photoshot; 68tr Nigel Blake (rspb-images.com); 69 www.johnmillerphotography.com; 70t AA; 70b AA/Michael Moody; 71tl Adrian Warren/www.lastrefuge.co.uk; 71tr AA/John Miller; 72tl Petworth House, Sussex/The Bridgeman Art Library; 72-73t AA/Peter Brown; 73bl Anthony Hatley/Alamy; 73br David Pearson/Alamy; 74 AF archive/Alamy; 75 AA/Michael Moody; 76-77 www.johnmillerphotography.com; 78 AA/Tom Mackie; 80-81 AA/Tom Mackie; 81bl Simon Finlay/Broads Authority; 82-83 Dick Flowers/Broads Authority; 83tl AA/Tom Mackie; 83tr AA/Tom Mackie; 84 AA/Tom Mackie; 85tl Simon Finlay/Broads Authority; 86tc Jeremy Early/FLPA; 86tr Chris Gomersall/Alamy; 86b AA/Tom Mackie; 87 AA/Tom Mackie; 88 Gary K Smith/FLPA; 89 Simon Finlay/Broads Authority; 90-91 AA/Tom Mackie; 90bl Broads Authority; 90bc AA/Wyn Voysey; 90br AA/Tom Mackie; 91bl AA/Tom Mackie; 92 AA/Tom Mackie; 94-95 AA/Tom Mackie; 94bl AA/Tom Mackie; 94br AA/Tom Mackie; 95bc AA/Tom Mackie; 95br Fred Hazelhoff/Foto Natura/FLPA; 96t AA/Tom Mackie; 96bl AA/Tom Mackie; 96bc AA/Tom Mackie; 96br AA/Tom Mackie; 97 AA/Tom Mackie; 99tl AA/Tom Mackie; 99tc AA/Tom Mackie; 99tr AA/Tom Mackie; 99b AA/Andy Midgley; 100-101 AA/Tom Mackie; 102 AA/Tom Mackie; 103bl AA/Tom Mackie; 103bc AA/Tom Mackie; 103br AA/Tom Mackie; 104t AA/M Birkitt; 104bl AA/Tom Mackie; 104br AA/Tom Mackie; 105 AA/Andy Midgley; 106 AA/Tom Mackie; 108-109 AA/Tom Mackie; 108bl AA/Tom Mackie; 108br AA/Tom Mackie; 109b AA/Tom Mackie; 111tl AA/Tom Mackie; 111tc AA/John Morrison; 111tr AA/Tom Mackie; 111b AA/Steve Day; 112 AA/Tom Mackie; 113tr AA/Tom Mackie; 113bl AA/Tom Mackie; 115tl AA/Tom Mackie; 114-115 AA/Tom Mackie; 116 AA/Tom Mackie; 116b AA/Tom Mackie; 117tl AA/Tom Mackie; 117tr AA/Tom Mackie; 118t R White, Yorkshire Dales National Park Authority; 118bl Andy Rouse/NHPA; 118br Paul Hobson/FLPA; 119 AA/Tom Mackie; 120 AA/Mike Kipling; 122-123 AA/Mike Kipling; 123t Bill Coster/NHPA; 124b AA/Mike Kipling; 125t AA/Mike Kipling; 125br AA/Mike Kipling; 126-127 AA/Mike Kipling; 126bl AA/Mike Kipling; 126br AA/Mike Kipling; 127bl AA/Mike Kipling; 127bc AA/Mike Kipling; 127br AA/Mike Kipling; 128 AA/Mike Kipling; 129 AA/Mike Kipling; 130-131 AA/Mike Kipling; 130b AA/John Morrison; 132t AA/Mike Kipling; 132bl AA/Mike Kipling; 132br AA/Mike Kipling; 133 AA/Mike Kipling; 134 AA/A Mockford & N Bonetti; 134-135t AA/A Mockford & N Bonetti; 137bl AA/A Mockford & N Bonetti; 139t AA/A Mockford & N Bonetti; 139bl AA/A Mockford & N Bonetti; 139br AA/A Mockford & N Bonetti; 140tl AA/A Mockford & N Bonetti; 140-141 AA/Tom Mackie; 140br AA/Tom Mackie; 142 AA/A Mockford & N Bonetti; 143tl Laurie Campbell; 143tc AA/A Mockford & N Bonetti; 143tr AA/A Mockford & N Bonetti; 144tl AA/A Mockford & N Bonetti; 144bl AA/A Mockford & N Bonetti; 144bc AA/A Mockford & N Bonetti; 144br AA/Tom Mackie; 145 AA/A Mockford & N Bonetti; 146-147 AA/Tom Mackie; 148 AA/Roger Coulam; 150 AA/Roger Coulam; 151 AA/Roger Coulam; 152 AA/Roger Coulam; 153 AA/Roger Coulam; 155tl AA/Roger Coulam; 155tc Laurie Campbell; 155tr AA/Roger Coulam; 155bl NTPL/Rupert Truman; 155br AA/Roger Coulam; 156-157 britainonview/ Duncan Davis; 158 AA/Jeff Beazley; 159bl Laurie Campbell; 159c AA/Roger Coulam; 159br Laurie Campbell; 160 Don Brownlow/Alamy; 161 Laurie Campbell; 162 AA/Chris Warren; 164-165 AA/Chris Warren; 164br AA/Chris Warren; 165bl AA/Michael Moody; 165br AA/Michael Moody; 166 AA/Chris Warren; 167t David Phillips/Pembrokeshire Coast National Park; 167b AA/Roger Coulam; 168-169 AA/Chris Warren; 168bl AA/Chris Warren; 168br AA/Chris Warren; 169bl Pembrokeshire County Council; 169bc AA/Chris Warren; 169br AA/Chris Warren; 170tl David Phillips/Pembrokeshire Coast National Park; 170tr AA/Nick Jenkins; 170b AA/Michael Moody; 171 AA/Chris Warren; 172tl AA/Chris Warren; 172-173 AA/Chris Warren; 172br AA/Nick Jenkins; 174 AA/Chris Warren; 175tl AA/Chris Warren; 175tr AA/Chris Warren; 175bl AA/Chris Warren; 175bc AA/Chris Warren; 175br AA/Chris Warren; 176 AA/Dan Santillo; 178-179 Philip Veale/Alamy; 178bl AA/Dan Santillo; 178br AA/Dan Santillo; 179bl AA/Dan Santillo; 180t AA/Nick Jenkins; 180-181 AA/Dan Santillo; 181tl AA/Dan Santillo; 182 AA/Dan Santillo; 183t AA/Nick Jenkins; 183bl AA/Dan Santillo; 183bc AA/Dan Santillo; 183br AA/Dan Santillo; 184 AA/Dan Santillo; 185 AA/Dan Santillo; 186-187 AA/Nick Jenkins; 188 AA/Nick Jenkins; 189 AA/Ian Burgum; 190 AA/Stephen Lewis; 192-193 Peter Lane/Photolibrary Wales; 192bl AA/Nick Jenkins; 192br AA/Steve Watkins; 193 AA/Stephen Lewis; 194 AA/Stephen Lewis; 194br AA/Richard Newton; 195tl AA/Steve Watkins; 195tr Michael Leach/NHPA; 197tl AA/Steve Watkins; 197tr AA; 197b AA/George Munday; 198-199 AA/Stephen Lewis; 200 AA/Stephen Lewis; 201 AA/Pat Aithie; 202 AA/Caroline Jones; 203bl AA/Steve Watkins; 203bc AA/Nick Jenkins; 203br AA/Stephen Lewis; 204 AA/David W Robertson; 206 AA/Steve Day; 207 AA/David W Robertson; 208 AA/David W Robertson; 209t AA/David W Robertson; 209bl AA/David W Robertson; 209bc AA/David W Robertson; 209br AA/David W Robertson; 210bl AA/David W Robertson; 210br AA/Sue Anderson; 211 AA/David W Robertson; 212 AA/David W Robertson; 213tl AA/David W Robertson; 213tr AA/David W Robertson; 214-215 AA/David W Robertson; 216tl AA/David W Robertson; 216tr AA/David W Robertson; 216b AA/David W Robertson; 217 AA/David W Robertson; ; 218 AA/Mark Hamblin; 220-221 AA/Mark Hamblin; 220bl AA/Mark Hamblin; 221bl AA/Mark Hamblin; 221bc Paul Hobson/Nature Picture Library; 221br AA/Mark Hamblin; 222 AA/Mark Hamblin; 222b AA/Mark Hamblin; 223 AA/Mark Hamblin; 225t Pete Cairns/Nature Picture Library; 225bl AA/Jonathan Smith; 225bc AA/Mark Hamblin; 225br AA/Jonathan Smith; 226 AA/Mark Hamblin; 227t AA/Mark Hamblin; 227bl AA/Jonathan Smith; 227bc AA/Mark Hamblin; 227br AA/Mark Hamblin; 228-229 AA/Mark Hamblin; 229b Tony Wright/earthscapes/Alamy; 230t Pete Cairns/Nature Picture Library; 230bl Desmond Dugan/FLPA; 230br AA/Jonathan Smith; 231 AA/Jonathan Smith; 232 Paul Lindsay/Alamy; 234tl Keith Shuttlewood/Alamy; 234tl AA/Chris Hill; 234tr Jeff Morgan tourism and leisure/Alamy; 234b AA/Max Jourdan; 235 AA/Max Jourdan; 236 AA/Roger Coulam.

Every effort has been made to trace the copyright holders, and we apologise in advance for any unintentional omissions or errors. We would be pleased to apply any corrections in any following edition of this publication.